THOMAS ROWLANDSON'S
DOCTOR SYNTAX DRAWINGS

Thomas Rowlandson's Doctor Syntax Drawings

An Introduction and Guide for Collectors

by

Jerold J. Savory

cygnus arts

London **Cygnus Arts**
Madison & Teaneck **Fairleigh Dickinson University Press**

**Published in the United Kingdom
by Cygnus Arts, a division of Golden Cockerel Press
16 Barter Street
London
WC1A 2AH**

**Published in the United States of America
by Fairleigh Dickinson University Press
Associated University Presses
440 Forsgate Drive
Cranbury
NJ 08512**

First published 1997

ISBN 1 900541 20 3

© 1997 Jerold J. Savory

British Library Cataloguing-in-Publication Data
Savory, Jerold J.
    Thomas Rowlandson's Doctor Syntax drawings : an introduction and guide for collectors
    1.Rowlandson, Thomas, 1756–1827 2.Prints, English – Collectors and collecting
    I.Title
    769.9'2
    ISBN 1900541203

Library of Congress Cataloguing-in-Publication Data
Rowlandson, Thomas. 1756–1827.
    [Doctor Syntax drawings]
    Thomas Rowlandson's Doctor Syntax drawings : an introduction and guide for
    collectors
/ Jerold J. Savory.
      p. cm.
    Includes bibliographical references and index.
    ISBN 0–8386–3746–9 (alk. paper)
    1. Combe, William. 1742–1823–Caricature and cartoons.
2. English wit and humor. Pictorial. I. Savory, Jerold J. II. Title.
NC1479.RBA4   1996
741.5'942–DC20

96–42290
CIP

Printed and bound in Kranj, Slovenia, by Gorenjski Tisk

For Aran and Vera and all that made you possible.

CONTENTS

ILLUSTRATIONS

THE THREE TOURS OF DOCTOR SYNTAX

THE TOUR OF DOCTOR SYNTAX IN SEARCH OF THE PICTURESQUE

THE SECOND TOUR OF DOCTOR SYNTAX, IN SEARCH OF CONSOLATION

THE THIRD TOUR OF DOCTOR SYNTAX, IN SEARCH OF A WIFE

ILLUSTRATIONS TO CHAPTERS 1 AND 3

APPENDIX TWO

FROM THE HISTORY OF JOHNNY QUÆ GENUS, THE LITTLE FOUNDLING OF THE LATE DOCTOR SYNTAX, 1821–22.

PREFACE

MY INTEREST IN THOMAS ROWLANDSON'S DRAWINGS HAS EVOLVED from my doctoral work at the University of Michigan and my teaching at Columbia College in South Carolina as a Victorian literature specialist. During a travel-study trip to the British Isles with my students, I discovered some delightful caricature prints from the late Victorian periodical *Vanity Fair* and purchased several. This led to some avid collecting and to publishing *The Vanity Fair Gallery: A Collector's Guide to the Caricatures* (1979) published by Associated University Presses with encouragement from the founding editor, Thomas Yoseloff.

As my interests broadened to include all caricature and cartooning of the Victorian period, Mr. Yoseloff and his son Julien encouraged me to publish *The Smiling Muse: Victoriana in the Comic Press* (1985), co-authored with Patricia Marks. I was now an avid collector of nineteenth-century popular art, especially comic drawings and caricatures. Therefore, during another trip with a student group in the later 1980s, I 'discovered' some Doctor Syntax prints in a London shop and was 'hooked'.

I could not find much readily available information about the Syntax prints, but I did learn about several print shops selling them in England and the United States. I also learned about the marvellous collections of Rowlandson drawings in the Huntington in California, and with a travel grant from Columbia College spent several days there seeing the Rowlandson collection and talking with the distinguished Rowlandson scholar, Dr. Robert Wark, who led me to the unpublished Stanford doctoral dissertation on Rowlandson and Doctor Syntax by one of his former students, Dr. Anthony Gully.

With help and encouragement from Dr. Wark, Dr. Gully and his excellent dissertation with its numerous leads, I started on my own research while continuing to collect the Syntax prints. For the time needed for my project, I am grateful to Columbia College and the Southern Regional Education Board for study grants. Bryan Sinclair, Columbia College reference librarian provided numerous leads and discoveries via his computer. Mary Gilkerson of the College's Art Department has been helpful with information and photography and I thank the College for a semester sabbatical to concentrate on research and writing.

Finally, I return to Thomas Yoseloff of Associated University Presses for continuing to have confidence in my work by recommending that this book be published through the alliance with London's Cygnus Arts and New Jersey's Fairleigh Dickinson University Press. Thanks especially to Andrew Lindesay for his editorial talents and creative directions in making this book among the first bearing the Cygnus Arts imprint.

I must add one more note. Thanks to my reference librarian friend, Bryan Sinclair, who discovered reference to a 1981 musical composition by John Joubert, *Dr. Syntax: Opus 85: A Suite for Recorder Ensemble*, and led me to a copy of a comic mystery novel entitled *Doctor Syntax* by Michael Petracca, published in 1991.

THOMAS ROWLANDSON'S
DOCTOR SYNTAX DRAWINGS

INTRODUCTION

ONE OF THE MOST POPULAR CHARACTERS IN NINETEENTH CENTURY English fiction, indeed the first popular fictional character to emerge from illustration, made his public debut in May 1809 in the first issue of *Poetical Magazine* under the editorial supervision of publisher and art dealer, Rudolph Ackermann (1764–1834). Under the title 'The Schoolmaster's Tour', the magazine featured its first instalment of the adventures and misadventures of the eccentric traveller, the pedantic cleric Doctor Syntax, illustrated with aquatint drawings by the prolific caricaturist and comic artist, Thomas Rowlandson (1756–1827), with narrative commentary in iambic tetrameter couplets by William Combe (1742–1823).

Each monthly issue of *Poetical Magazine* from May 1809 to May 1811 contained one or two of Rowlandson's illustrations. The project was so successful that in 1812, Ackermann put together a book, the first of what would be several editions and re-issuings, under the title, *Doctor Syntax In Search of the Picturesque,* featuring thirty of Rowlandson's drawings. By 1820, the book had gone through five editions and four re-issuings, prompting the enterprising editor to continue the story in a sequel in his magazine, immediately put into book form at the end of the year under the title, *Doctor Syntax in Search of Consolation.* Once again, success stimulated yet another sequel in 1821 entitled *Doctor Syntax in Search of a Wife* with twenty-five more plates, bringing the total of Rowlandson drawings in the three tours to eighty, the largest number he had done for any of the numerous books he illustrated.

In the following chapters, I will provide more detailed information on the Rowlandson-Combe-Ackermann collaboration, the background contexts that gave rise to the Syntax character and the enormous public reception that led to additional Syntax-related books, some illustrated by Rowlandson, some copied by later and less-talented artists and numerous other memorabilia reflecting Doctor Syntax's rise to the status of a Victorian folk hero.

Although editions of the *Three Tours* appeared up until 1903, most of those from 1868 on are obviously copies of Rowlandson's work, sometimes with "After

Rowlandson" properly noted. During the twentieth century, the series has never been reprinted in its entirety, even though appreciative examples have been included in several studies of Rowlandson, as noted in the Bibliography. Therefore, this book reproduces all of the Rowlandson drawings from the *Three Tours*, taken from the earliest editions between 1812 and 1820.

Since my primary purpose is the focus upon the Rowlandson drawings rather than Combe's lengthy narrative text, I have provided just enough of a summary of his narration, including selected lines for each drawing, to give readers a sense of what is going on in the drawing. While I hope that the book may hold some interest for those interested in art, literature, and popular culture of the nineteenth century, I am especially hopeful that it may provide collectors or potential collectors of the Doctor Syntax prints with some useful information. I have, therefore, included a section especially for collectors on locating and identifying various editions of books with Rowlandson illustrations, as well as the prints, usually taken from the books and sold individually. I have also added a note about other Syntax collectibles for those who are fortunate enough to come upon them.

Although I have included a selected and annotated bibliography, I am especially grateful for the books on Rowlandson by Robert R. Wark and John Hayes and have relied heavily upon Harlan Hamilton's *Doctor Syntax: A Silhouette of William Combe, Esq.* (London: Chatto & Windus, 1969) and Anthony L. Gully's excellent unpublished doctoral dissertation, 'Thomas Rowlandson's Doctor Syntax' (Stanford University, 1972). Dr. Gully's study is the most thorough examination of the Combe-Rowlandson collaboration. I appreciate both his insights and his encouragement as I decided to undertake this book.

CHAPTER ONE

THE 'DOCTOR SYNTAX'
COLLABORATION

T HE NAME 'DOCTOR SYNTAX' IS SYNONYMOUS WITH THE PEDANTIC AND eccentric schoolmaster who captured the affections of readers for nearly a century. Although the main purpose of this book is to reproduce the delightful Rowlandson prints for a contemporary audience over a century removed from Dr. Syntax's nineteenth-century heyday, a few comments are in order about Syntax's origins and the remarkable trio that brought him to life.

Rudolph Ackermann was born in Saxony in 1764, the son of a harness maker and coach builder. After studying coach designing in Paris, he settled in London where he distinguished himself at this craft until well into the 1800s. However, in 1795, his interests shifted to fine arts collecting and publishing and to bookselling, along with his numerous humanitarian projects. He was clearly an enterprising businessman and mediator capable of bringing together the divergent talents and personalities of writer William Combe and artist Thomas Rowlandson.

Thomas Rowlandson was born in London in 1756, the son of a textile merchant who subsequently went bankrupt and died in 1764, leaving Thomas in the care of his aunt. He studied at the Royal Academy and went to Paris during the early 1770s. His first exhibition was at the Royal Academy in 1775. He inherited a substantial sum from an aunt and during the remaining years of the eighteenth century, he travelled extensively, keeping a written record of his journeys. His association with Ackermann began in the late 1790s.

Rowlandson had already distinguished himself as a caricaturist and illustrator, having done the illustrations for Henry Fielding's *Tom Jones* and *Joseph Andrews,* Oliver Goldsmith's *The Vicar of Wakefield,* Laurence Sterne's *Tristram Shandy* and Tobias Smollet's *Humphrey Clinker, Roderick Random* and *Peregrine Pickle.* By the time that Ackermann was ready to launch his new *Poetical Magazine,* he had no doubt about his choice of illustrator. He proposed to Rowlandson that each issue would present to capture the public's interest in a serialised story, written in verse and illustrated in colour. Rowlandson agreed, already having some ideas about a main character. Ackermann's next move was to secure his writer. William Combe

Fig. 1. 'With no less fury did Mrs. Partridge fly on the poor pedagogue. Her tongue, teeth, and hands fell upon him at once.' Illustration by Thomas Rowlandson to *Tom Jones* by Henry Fielding.

was not only a likely prospect but was also near at hand, serving time for his debts nearby in King's Bench Prison where he was while continuing to write.

William Combe was born in 1741 into the middle class family of an iron-monger. However, he was brought up as a gentleman, with an education at Eton and at Oxford University from which he left without completing his degree. Thanks to an indulgent uncle, he was able to round out his education with several years of travel in France and Italy. Clever, bright and handsome, Combe moved effortlessly into society circles as a showy and well-dressed celebrity and conver-sationalist. Although he drank nothing but water until his final years when wine was prescribed for his health, he enjoyed gaming and living in the manner of wealthy aristocrats whom he befriended and who recognised him as 'Count Combe'. When his inheritance ran out, he turned to writing for a living and although he quickly became well-known, he refused to sign his numerous publi-cations so that his friends would not know that he wrote for money. Nevertheless, he became one of England's best-paid and most productive hackwriters for nearly a half century, freelancing in political journalism, history, editing and verse satire.

Unfortunately, his spending and his debts caught up with him and he was sent him to prison several times, where he spent most of the last fifteen years of his life.

Fig. 2. 'Humphrey Clinker introduced to the Bramble family.' Illustration by Thomas Rowlandson to *Humphrey Clinker* by Tobias Smollett (from the 1793 two-volume edition).

However, while an inmate, he continued to draw upon his accounts and to write. It was in King's Bench prison where Ackermann and Combe reached a gentleman's agreement (involving a drawing account, rather than salary) for several projects, including the comic verse to accompany Rowlandson's drawings for Ackermann's new monthly magazine.

These, then, were the three men jointly responsible for the creation of Doctor Syntax. Although Combe and Rowlandson were considerably different from one another in age and temperament, they did share a capacity for turning out great quantities of work in their respective writing and drafting. Ackermann was well suited to serve as intermediary between them. Their working relationship is described by Combe in his preface to the second edition (1812) of *The Tour of Doctor Syntax in Search of the Picturesque*:

> The *designs* to which this volume is so greatly indebted, I was informed would follow in a series, and it was proposed to me to share out a story from them. An etching or a drawing was accordingly sent to me every month, and I composed a certain proportion of pages in verse, in which, of course, the subject of the design was included: the rest depended upon what my imagination could furnish. When the first print was sent to me, I did not know what would be the subject

of the second; and in this manner, in a great measure, the artist continued designing, and I continued writing every month for two years, 'till a work containing nearly ten thousand lines was produced: the artist and the writer having no personal communication with, or knowledge of each other.

By the time Ackermann approached Rowlandson with his plans for the new *Poetical Magazine*, the artist had already showed him some drawings representing an old clergyman and schoolmaster who fancied himself a writer, artist and musician, travelling quixotically during his holidays in search of the picturesque. Rowlandson had been experimenting with a character resembling Syntax when he discussed the pending project with his long-time friend, schoolmate and travel companion, the three-hundred-pound comedic actor John Bannister, who apparently offered himself as a model. Rowlandson had a totally different type in mind who was, in Bannister's words, "a skin and bone hero, a pedantic old prig in a shovel hat with a pony, sketching tools and rattletraps, and place him in such scrapes as travellers frequently meet with—hedge alehouses, second and third-rate inns, thieves, gibbets, mad bulls, and the like".

Two other persons deserve mention for their influence on the Syntax series. William Gilpin (1742–1804) clearly influenced Combe's text with its gentle satire on picturesque theories. Like Syntax, Gilpin was a travelling cleric-schoolmaster who wrote and sketched on his travels in the Lake District, Wales and Scotland. According to the *Dictionary of National Biography*, Gilpin, through his books on how to identify and delight in the pastoral and gothic scenes, created "a new class of travellers". A virtual cult of the picturesque sprang up around him, sparked by the popular fiction of such gothic novelists as Charlotte Smith and Mrs. Ann Ward Radcliffe. However, as Anthony Gully convincingly argues, picturesque satire may have been Combe's intent but not Rowlandson's.[1]

The second influence upon Rowlandson, and one with greater impact, was the caricaturist George Woodward (?1760–1809) who, following the lead of Bunbury, introduced a format for depicting episodic development of a pictorial story, apparently a forerunner of our modern cartoon strip. Woodward's *Eccentric Excursions* (1808) is a comic travel book with letterpress poking fun at the picturesque extravagances of Gilpin. It is the illustrated scenes themselves that give the book its unique character and appeal. In the tradition of Hogarth and Gillray, he would contrast the boney country vicar to the overfed bishop and would often use clergy as foils to young women, as did Rowlandson. From 1792, through the remaining years of Woodward's life, Rowlandson collaborated with him on a dozen or more books with Rowlandson working from Woodward's designs.

Fig. 3. Two drawings by William Gilpin, showing variations on shading. Compare to Rowlandson's drawings in plates 13 and 18.

Clearly, the idea for the Syntax character had been growing in Rowlandson's mind for some time prior to Ackermann's request. Well before 1809, he had been drawing satirical characters to poke fun at what he saw as pedantic and self-righteous behaviour, frequently depicted as clerics and sometimes with bawdy and erotic sketches.

Many of these previously successful caricatures and comic illustrations appeared in broadsheets, periodicals and books. Through these he developed the character of a pedantic but likeable and worldly schoolmaster-cleric to follow the misadventures and mishaps as well as joys of life on the road. Other famous fictional characters of the day, such as Fielding's Parson Adams in *Joseph Andrews* and Doctor Primrose in Goldsmith's *Vicar of Wakefield*, share Syntax's perilous adventures and a passion for writing about them; but neither shares his interest in young ladies and carousing, sport and hunting, gaming and the theatre. Rowlandson's Syntax clearly has his own special character, frequently in contrast to Combe's more reserved narrative, tempered to avoid offending the clergy, as noted in prefatory remarks published in his last work, *Letters to Marianne* of 1823, the year of his death:

> When I began my Doctor Syntax, I had the designs of the artist laid before me; and the task prescribed to me was, to write up to them. Those designs might have been applied to a satire upon the national clergy; but if ridicule was the intention, to such a plan I resolved not to lend my pen: I respect the clergy; and I determined to turn the edge of the weapon which I thought was levelled against them.[2]

As Gully notes, "Though many of the Syntax drawings with slightly erotic overtones may have been made for private sale, or Rowlandson's own amusement, it seems quite possible that Combe may have chosen not to write verses around some, thus excluding them from the last two *Tours*."[3] Gully refers to the last two tours for which, unlike the first, Rowlandson's drawings were in response to Combe's narrative. In using his verses as a platform for his own ideas and literary theories, Combe presents Syntax as far more dull and long-winded than Rowlandson's visualisation would suggest. Thus, it is reasonable for our purposes to present the drawings with only brief excerpts from Combe's text, some of which lapses into doggerel as well as misses the humour of the drawings.

Doctor Syntax is presented by Rowlandson as more than just a simple and humorous eccentric: he is writer, musician, artist and sportsman. However, it is as a traveller that Syntax reflects Rowlandson's main focus in the *Tours*. Travel books enjoyed great popularity, even long before the *Tours* were published.[4] The Lake District was becoming an increasingly popular attraction, as were the great country houses, such as Eaton, the newly-opened spas, the theatres such as Covent Garden and even budding urban industrial sites such as Liverpool. Although a few of Rowlandson's scenes deal directly with Combe's stress on satirising the picturesque, Rowlandson's own focus is on satirising popular travel books and travellers, as the commentaries on certain of the plates will show.

As a comic traveller, Syntax becomes a unique contribution within a literary tradition beginning with the lanky and whimsical Don Quixote of La Mancha and his tubby, unimaginative companion Sancho Panza in Cervantes's *Don Quixote*. This parallel becomes even more obvious in the *Second Tour* in which Syntax's companion is the Irish footman Pat. This is all in the tradition of the picaresque, one which involves a central hero-adventurer who provides the link between otherwise disparate episodes. Rowlandson's public was well aware of the popular French novel, *Gil Blas*, Alain René Le Sage's story tracing the adventures of the wandering hero. They would also know of Fielding's *Tom Jones* and Smollett's *Peregrine Pickle*, both in the picaresque tradition. Also, an earlier verse satire, *Hudibras* by Samuel Butler, presented the woeful misadventures of the Presbyterian colonel Hudibras, accompanied by his squire Ralpho, in his attempt to win a widow and her highly desirable property. In fact, Combe borrowed Butler's doggerel verse scheme for his own metrics in the three tours of Doctor Syntax.

Wherever Rowlandson got his original idea for Syntax, and there are probably several inspirational sources, he produced a memorable character, the first fictional hero to have emerged from book illustration. His drawings stand on their own comic merits, not merely as embellishments of the text. He is able to tell whole stories in a single drawing or in paired drawings or ones in series. He does not resort to the exaggeration of caricature, nor does he engage Doctor Syntax in fantastic adventures for effect. The Doctor's social predicaments and social blunders are enough to maintain the reader's interest from drawing to drawing.

This, then, was the collaboration that produced Doctor Syntax, who became "Rowlandson's greatest hit", to quote one of the artist's most prominent scholars and biographers, John Hayes.[5]

The next section of this book contains all of Rowlandson's drawings for the Three Tours. The following chapters and appendices contain further commentary on the publishing history of the Syntax books under the Ackermann-Rowlandson-Combe collaboration, Syntax-related publications by other writers and artists and an array of additional memorabilia, all of which may be of interest to potential collectors. Chapter Four also provides advice for those beginning a collection.

CHAPTER TWO

THE 'DOCTOR SYNTAX' TOURS

THIS CHAPTER CONTAINS THE ILLUSTRATIONS TO THE THREE TOURS OF Doctor Syntax, *The Tour of Doctor Syntax in Search of the Picturesque*, *The Second Tour of Dr. Syntax, in Search of Consolation* and *The Third Tour of Dr. Syntax, in Search of a Wife*. The drawings speak eloquently for themselves, and careful observation of Rowlandson's details often provides additional touches of more subtle humour. The text accompanying each plate is intended to provide the narrative context, comments on the scenes, notes on Rowlandson's designs and several lines from Combe's verse that most closely relate to that drawing. The original aquatint drawings measure about 5" x 7", with a few variations.

The first section contains the drawings from the first of the three tours, *Doctor Syntax in Search of the Picturesque*. In this group, Rowlandson provided all of the drawings first and Combe wrote the letterpress in response to them. The action in the first tour covers about eight weeks. Syntax travels by way of Oxford to York, where he is the guest of Squire Hearty, then on to visit Lord Carlisle at Castle Howard in Yorkshire (Carlisle had been Combe's contemporary at Eton). Lord Carlisle agrees to become the patron for Syntax's projected book and invites Syntax to visit him in London. He travels to Keswick in the Lake District, where he meets the delightful Squire Worthy and his charming family. After a few days, he journeys to Liverpool and then by a wandering route to London where he spends two weeks in Lord Carlisle's townhouse while finishing his book and arranging for its publication.

He then returns home, which is probably somewhere in Yorkshire. On his way, Syntax becomes lost, is attacked by robbers and saved by damsels, loses his horse and finds her again, is overcharged in an inn, is attacked by a bull, is the brunt of a joke that leads him to mistake a 'gentleman's house' for an inn, plays his fiddle for dancers, reads his tour and preaches a sermon to sleeping auditors, and, after more adventures in London, returns home with a published book, a new position and a delighted wife who takes off with him for his new job in the Lake District.

The Second Tour of Dr. Syntax, in Search of Consolation, begins with the death and funeral of his wife and his subsequent journey with his Irish horseman and companion, Pat. This tour takes him to Eaton Hall in Cheshire, to Ludlow and to Bath. He is introduced to a jovial ceremony called 'Skimmington', visits Lady Bounty where he is attacked by bees and where he lectures to young women at a seminary. He conducts a wedding, makes return visits to Oxford and London, discusses publishing a sequel to his book, and returns to Worthy Hall in time for the celebration of Miss Worthy's marriage.

The Third Tour of Dr. Syntax, in Search of a Wife, includes several scenes where courtship advice and prospects are given to him. He takes matters into his own hands in meeting a rather wide variety of available ladies such as Widow Omicron, Miss Crotchet of Tulip Hall, Widow Horner, Lady Macnight the Astronomer, Mrs. Brisket and the artist Miss Pallet. He discovers a foundling left on his doorstep and, finding his bride, he marries. After two happy years of marriage and raising the foundling, he dies.

I

THE TOUR OF
DOCTOR SYNTAX
IN SEARCH OF
THE PICTURESQUE

1. FRONTISPIECE. THE REV. DOCTOR SYNTAX.

Rowlandson introduces Doctor Syntax at his favourite study chair with a folio of picturesque scenes on his desk. Combe's verse tells of the schoolmaster's meditation on the ending of another school year:

The School was done, the bus'ness o'er,
When, tir'd of Greek and Latin lore,
Good Syntax sought his easy chair,
And sat in calm composure there.
His wife was to a neighbour gone,
To hear the chit-chat of the town;
And left him the unfrequent power
Of brooding thro' a quiet hour.
Thus, while he sat, a busy train
Of images besieged his brain.
Of Church-preferment he had none;
Nay, all his hope of that was gone.
He felt that he content must be
With drudging in a Curacy.

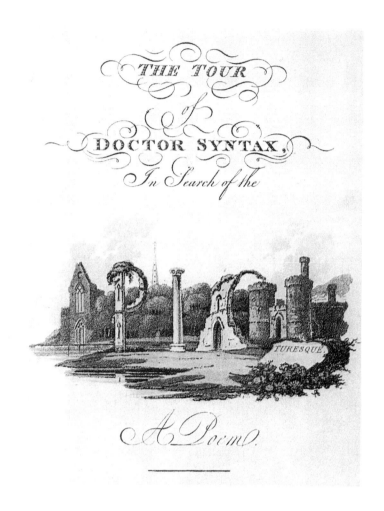

2. TITLE PAGE. *THE TOUR OF DOCTOR SYNTAX IN SEARCH OF THE PICTURESQUE*

The title page itself is a significant satirical drawing with the word 'picturesque' spelled out in Gothic ruins. This is a spoof on the contemporary artists and writers who went to absurd lengths to create such landscape effects, sometimes lavishing attention upon gothic architecture, intact or in ruins, to create an atmosphere of mystery or horror. Such depictions of ruins were widely popular at the time.

One problem preoccupying Doctor Syntax is how to raise money to pay the increasing taxes and food bills for his school, as well as for his wife's demanding tastes:

Good Mrs. Syntax was a lady
Ten years, perhaps, beyond her hey-day;
But tho' the blooming charms had flown

That grac'd her youth; it still was known
The love of power she never lost,
And Syntax found it to his cost.

3. DR. SYNTAX SETTING OUT.

Resolved to set out on a tour of the Lake District to write and sketch his picturesque adventures, Syntax draws on his riding gloves in preparation for mounting his nag Grizzle, held by his indifferent stableman. Curious villagers look on as the departing traveller ignores his wife's parting advice:

> At length the ling'ring moment came
> That gave the dawn of wealth and fame.
> Incurious Ralph, exact at four,
> Led Grizzle, saddled, to the door;
> And soon, with more than common state,
> The Doctor stood before the gate.

4. DR. SYNTAX LOSING HIS WAY.

Not far into his journey, he comes upon a defaced and confusing guidepost, and decides to take advantage of the situation and sketch the 'uninforming piece of wood':

Upon that bank awhile I'll sit,
And let poor Grizzle graze a bit;
But, as my time shall not be lost,
I'll make a drawing of the post;
And, tho' your flimsy taste may flout it,
There's something picturesque about it.

5. DR. SYNTAX STOPPED BY HIGHWAYMEN.

Soon after, he faces another delay by robbers who take his money and tie him to a tree:

> For now, with fierce impetuous rush,
> Three ruffians issued from a bush;
> One Grizzle stopp'd, and seiz'd the reins,
> While they all threat the Doctor's brains.
> Poor Syntax, trembling with afright,
> Resists not such superior might,
> But yields to them their savage pleasure,
> And gives his purse, with all its treasure.

6.   DR. SYNTAX BOUND TO A TREE BY HIGHWAYMEN.

All is not lost as two passing damsels rescue and feed the distressed traveller:

> Nor did La Mancha's val'rous knight
> Feel greater pleasure at the sight,
> When, overwhelm'd with love and awe,
> His Dulcinea first he saw:
> For on two trotting palfreys came,
> And each one bore a comely dame . . .
> . . . When each leap'd quickly from her steed,
> To join in charitable deed.
> They drew their knives to cut the noose,
> And let the mournful pris'ner loose.

Nor is his money supply gone since Mrs. Syntax has sewn banknotes to his coat lining.

7. DR. SYNTAX DISPUTING HIS BILL
WITH THE LANDLADY.

His faithful nag Grizzle, lost in the robbery fiasco, returns, but with her tail and ears cut by the thieves. Leaving the horse in the care of the ostler, Syntax finds room and meals at the Crown Royal Inn, only to discover that he has been overcharged:

SYNTAX: The paper fills me with a:right;
          I surely do not read it right:
          For, at the bottom here I see
          Th' enormous total—one pound, three!
LADY: The charges all are fairly made,
          If you will eat, I must be paid.

8. DR. SYNTAX COPYING THE WIT OF THE WINDOW.

Settling his bill for half the amount, he resumes his travels on his patched-up Grizzle. At the next inn, he is fascinated by the stories of joys and woes he imagines on the walls and windows. Thus, he decides to capture them in prose:

> The window quickly caught his eye,
> On whose clean panes he could descry
> The motley works of many a Muse.
> There was enough to pick and choose . . .

However, Rowlandson has added a comic touch missed by Combe. The distracted maidservant, Dolly, spills her boiling water on the Doctor. Combe's narrative has the water "filling both his shoes". However, Rowlandson's drawing makes it quite clear that this is not the direction of the scalding stream!

9. DR. SYNTAX ENTERTAINED AT COLLEGE.

After bestowing a grateful kiss on the chambermaid who attends to his scalds, Syntax journeys on to Oxford, his *alma mater*, to see his old friend Dicky Bend, now Provost of his college, and tell him of his dream to write and illustrate a travel book:

Such is the book I mean to make,
And I've no doubt the work will take:
For tho' your wisdom may decry it,
The simple folk will surely buy it.
I will allow it is but trash,
But then it furnishes the cash . . .

Behold the dishes due appear—
Fish in the van, beef in the rear;
But he who the procession led,
By some false step or awkward tread,
Or curs'd by some malignant pow'r,
Fell headlong on the marble floor!

10. DR. SYNTAX PURSUED BY A BULL.

In a pasture overlooking the Oxford turrets, Syntax begins to sketch. However:

> A wicked bull no sooner view'd him,
> Than loud he roar'd, and straight pursued him.
> The Doctor finding danger near,
> Flew swiftly on the wings of Fear,
> And nimbly clamber'd up a tree,
> That gave him full security.
> But as he ran to save his bacon,
> By hat and wig he was forsaken;
> His sketch-book too he left behind,
> A prey to the unlucky wind;
> While Grizzle, startled by the rout,
> Broke from the hedge, and pranc'd about.

11. DR. SYNTAX MISTAKES A GENTLEMAN'S HOUSE FOR AN INN.

The next stop is Welcome Hall where Squire Bounty invites the Doctor to free room and board, a clergy special. Accepting like a Lord, Syntax proceeds to get "lordly drunk":

> He rang the bell and call'd the waiters,
> To take his shoes off, and his gaiters.
> "Go tell the maid to shew the bed,
> Where I may lay my aching head.
> Here, take my wig, and bring a cap.
> My eyelids languish for a nap."

Little does Syntax realise that Squire Bounty and his friends have been playing a joke on the travelling cleric by placing him in a 'Gentleman's House', rather than an inn. The Squire and his party arrive to let Syntax in on the joke.

12. DOCTOR SYNTAX MEDITATING ON THE TOMBS.

Passing a churchyard on his way to his next inn, Syntax pauses, hoping to be inspired by the "sepulchral ground" and maybe a "chatty ghost" or two. He does find a grave-digging sexton who provides him with extended dialogue on death, the dead and their epitaphs. Standing on a tomb, Syntax holds his sketchbook behind his back, waiting for the right moment to capture this Gothic scene, complete with the graves, the praying woman, the angelic children and the old man who listens intently:

SYNTAX: We both, my friend, pursue one trade;
I for the living, you the dead.
For whom that grave do you prepare,
With such keen haste, and cheerful air.

SEXTON: And please your Revrence, Lawyer Thrust,
Thank Heav'n, will moulder here to dust:
Never before did I take measure
Of any grave with half the pleasure.

13. DOCTOR SYNTAX TUMBLING INTO THE WATER.

Learning that a riverside castle had just been hit by lightning, so reducing it to ruins, Syntax decides to sketch this ready-made Gothic scene, only to stumble into the river:

A heap of stones the Doctor found,
Which loosely lay upon the ground,
To form a seat, where he might trace
The antique beauty of the place:
But, while his eye observ'd the line
That was to limit the design,
The stones gave way, and sad to tell,
Down from the bank he headlong fell.

14. DOCTOR SYNTAX LOSES HIS MONEY ON THE RACE-GROUND.

Near York, Syntax comes upon a horse race and learns how to place a bet—to his disadvantage:

> He got advice. The sport began;
> The jockies whipp'd, the horses ran,—
> And, when the coursers reach'd their post,
> The man scream'd out—"Your horse has lost!"

15. DOCTOR SYNTAX AT A REVIEW.

At York, he stays with the congenial Squire Hearty who becomes his guide to a military review:

> And e'er they pass'd a mile or two,
> Beheld the scene of the review.
> The troops drawn up in proud array
> An animating sight display:
> The well-form'd squadrons wheel around.
> The standards wave, the trumpets sound.

A brief comment on Grizzle provides a nice added touch:

> When Grizzle, long matur'd to war,
> And not without an honour'd scar,
> Found all her former spirits glow
> As when she used to meet the foe:
> No ears she prick'd, for she had none:
> Nor cock'd her tail, for that was gone;
> But still she snorted, foam'd, and flounced;
> Then up she rear'd, and off she bounc'd.

16. DOCTOR SYNTAX WITH MY LORD.

Syntax shares Squire Hearty's dinner table, surrounded by his prized gallery. The theme of scholars enjoying drinks and cigars while discussing books, arts and current events is frequently to be found in Rowlandson's work. Here it is given an added comic twist as the lordly connoisseur converses with the hungry traveller:

MY LORD: What think you, Doctor, of the show
             Of pictures that around you glow?
SYNTAX: I'll by-and-by enjoy the treat:
             But now, my Lord, I'd rather eat.

17. DOCTOR SYNTAX MADE FREE OF THE CELLAR.

Next, the generous Squire invites Syntax to his wine and beer cellar where he is free
to partake at his pleasure:

> Whene'er a stranger guest we see,
> To make him of the cellar free.
> To you the same respect we bear,
> And therefore beg to lead you there;
> Where ev'ry noble butt doth claim
> The honour of some titled name.
> The servants waited on the stairs
> With cautious form and humble airs.

18. DOCTOR SYNTAX SKETCHING THE LAKE.

Near Keswick in the Lake District, Syntax finds a scene ideally suited for his picturesque masterpiece; and Rowlandson finds a delightful opportunity for a visual sending-up of the theories of the picturesque, especially those of Gilpin. In contrast to the dull-witted fisherman puzzled by the the cleric with his sketching pad, Syntax takes in the placid lake scene, complete with boating party, intently. Unfortunately, Grizzle is also tempted by the sylvan scene:

> Soon as the morn began to break,
> Old Grizzle bore him to the lake;
> Along the banks he gravely pac'd,
> And all its various beauties trac'd.
> But Grizzle, in her haste to pass,
> Lur'd by a tempting tuft of grass,
> A luckless step now chanc'd to take,
> And sous'd the Doctor in the lake.

19. DOCTOR SYNTAX SKETCHING AFTER NATURE.

Rowlandson continues his satirising of current theories of the picturesque which promoted the pictorial qualities of placid farm animals, including rustic cart horses. In this delightful drawing, the animals are anything but placid as they join in what seems to be a choral performance for the puzzled artist. Grizzle stands in the background, looking more indifferent than placid, and the dog has something more important on his mind than posing for a portrait. In contrast to the animated animal entourage, Squire Worthy with his wife and sister stand placidly amused by their sketching guest, and the old woman in the doorway seems to share Rowlandson's joke. Combe comments:

A tub inverted, form'd his seat;   The Doctor now, with genius big,
The animals their painter meet: First drew a cow, and next a pig:
Cows, asses, sheep, and ducks and geese,   A sheep now on the paper passes,
Present themselves, to grace the piece;   And then he sketch'd a group of asses;
Poor Grizzle, too, among the rest.   Nor did he fail to do his duty
Of the true picturesque possest . . .   In giving Grizzle all her beauty.

20. DOCTOR SYNTAX ROBBED OF HIS PROPERTY.

At a crowded inn, Syntax is forced to share a room with a man who tries to rob him—
unsuccessfully:

> He gently seiz'd the fancied store;
> But as he pass'd the creaking door,
> Syntax awoke, and saw the thief.
> When loudly bawling for relief,
> He forward rush'd in naked state
> And caught the culprit at the gate.
> Against that gate his head he beat,
> Then kick'd him headlong to the street.

21. DR. SYNTAX SELLS GRIZZLE.

Actually, he *attempts* to sell her:

> The morrow came, and thro' the fair
> The Farmer led the grizzle mare.
> Says one, "I would not bid a pound;
> She's only fit to feed a hound."

However, Rowlandson's delight in drawing horses does not end with Grizzle's temporary disappearance from her final sale at a much-reduced price. She shows up later in the care of her former owner who 'marries' her to his breeder Match'em, thus providing a happy ending to Grizzle's role in the cleric's adventures.

22. RURAL SPORTS.

Coming upon a peasant village festivity, the multi-talented schoolmaster agrees to substitute for the drunken fiddler, joining in the fun:

'Twas thus they fiddled, danc'd, and sung:
With harmless glee the village rung.
At length dull Midnight bid them close
A day of joy with calm repose.

23. DR. SYNTAX WITH THE DAIRY MAID.

In a mock-sentimental scene, Syntax, attracted by a "village damsel young and fair," offers some free 'counselling' for the weeping milkmaid:

> "Come here, sweet girl," he softly said;
> "Tell me your cares—nor be afraid:
> Come here, and seat you by my side;
> You'll find in me a friendly guide."

However, Syntax's offers of "friendliness" are soon dampened:

> The list'ning mother, who had heard
> Love talk'd of, kindled at the word;
> And, rushing in, express'd her rage:
> "For shame! For shame! while hoary age
> Whitens your head, I see your eye
> Is beaming with iniquity . . .
> A Parson too! may Heaven forgive
> The wicked age in which we live!"

24. DR. SYNTAX AT LIVERPOOL.

Syntax's visit to Liverpool gives Rowlandson a chance to draw the newly-built
Exchange Building:

> Tho' we in holy Scripture read
> That Tyre and Sidon did exceed
> In wealth, the cities of the world,
> Where ships their wand'ring sails unfurl'd;
> That e'en her merchants bore the bell
> In eating and in drinking well;
> Were richer than the lordly great,
> And vy'd with princes in their state;
> Yet, with all their power and rule,
> I think that they ne'er went to school
> In such a 'Change as Liverpool.

25. DR. SYNTAX READING HIS TOUR.

Seated in a country inn and urged to read from his manuscript, Syntax proudly obliges and promptly puts his audience to sleep, save for two lovers in the background with other interests. Syntax begins his performance with a lengthy passage on the beauties of nature, tapping his foot to keep rhythm:

> But, as he read, tho' full of grace,
> Tho' strong expression mark'd his face,
> Tho' his feet struck the sounding floor,
> And his voice thunder'd thro' the door,
> Each hearer as th' infection crept
> O'er the numb'd sense, unconscious slept!
> One dropp'd his pipe, another snor'd,
> The bed of down an oaken board:
> The cobbler yawn'd, then sunk to rest,
> His chin reclining on his breast.

26. SYNTAX PREACHING.

In a print appropriately paired with the previous one, the wandering cleric is invited
to preach in a country church where, once again, he puts his listeners to sleep, this
time with an extended message from The Book of Job on human misery!

> He said, as he'd been us'd to teaching,
> He'd give them half an hour's preaching.
> This was accepted with a smile,
> And they then strutted up the aisle;
> When, in due time, and with due grace,
> Syntax display'd his preaching face.
> And, in bold tones, tho' somewhat hoarse,
> He gave the following discourse:
> "The subject I shall now rehearse
> Is JOB the fifth, the seventh verse."

27. DR. SYNTAX AND THE BOOKSELLER.

The scene now shifts from the country to London after several events described in Combe's text, including Grizzle's return with ears and tail now healed and Syntax's dropping her to go on to the city by stagecoach. As a guest of his influential patron, Lord Carlisle, in his London townhouse, Syntax busies himself completing his manuscript. He arranges for its publication with Vellum, the ignorant but hard-headed and arrogant bookseller and publisher:

> VELLUM: I wish to know, Sir, what you mean
> by kicking up, Sir, such a scene?
> And who you are, Sir, and your name,
> And on what errand here you came?
>
> SYNTAX: My errand was to bid you look
> With care and candour on this Book;
> And tell me whether you think fit
> To buy, or print, or publish it?

Vellum's initial resistance is softened when he sees Lord Carlisle's letter of commendation.

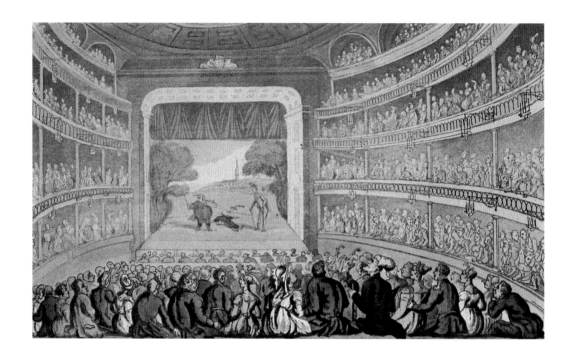

28. DR. SYNTAX AT COVENT GARDEN THEATRE.

After arrangements for publication have been agreed, Syntax obliges Lord Carlisle's request to tell him the story of his life. This gives Syntax a chance to speak at length (at one point, even falling asleep himself during the telling!) about his childless marriage, his travels since leaving home, and his views on literature and literary critics. Since Syntax had not visited London for twenty years, he takes a tour of the city and attends a Covent Garden play. Combe's verse echoes contemporary satires of Alexander Pope and John Dryden:

He hasten'd to the Playhouse door
And took his place within the pit,
Beside a critic and a wit,
As wits and critics now are known
To hash up nonsense for the Town . . .
In former times none went to see
The mere effects of scenery,

The constant laugh, the forc'd grimace,
The vile distortion's of the face.
In those good times none went to see
Pierots and Clowns in Comedy.
Men sought perfection to discern,
And learned critics went to learn.

29. THE DOCTOR'S DREAM.

Following his book deal with Vellum and his conversation at the theatre, Syntax dozes off while browsing in Lord Carlisle's library. His dream recalls Jonathan Swift's 'Battle of the Books', Pope's 'Essay on Criticism' and skirmishes between the classics and the mass-produced writing of hacks:

> That I was in the Strand I dream'd,
> And o'er my head methought there seem'd,
> A flight of volumes in the air,
> In various bindings gilt and fair:
> The unfolded leaves, expos'd to view,
> Serv'd them as wings on which they flew.

30. DR. SYNTAX RETURNED FROM HIS TOUR.

After a few days of detours with the reclaimed Grizzle on his homeward route, Syntax arrives home to an impatient wife (and dog) who chastises him even before he has a chance to light his pipe (which, in a long soliloquy on smoking, he calls his "social tube"):

> He sat him down his pipe to smoke,
> Look'd sad, and not a word he spoke;
> But Madam soon her speech began,
> And in discordant tones it ran:
> "I think by that confounded look,
> You have not writ your boasted book.
> Yes, all your money you have spent
> And come back poorer than you went."

However, once Syntax tells her of his success, she smothers him with affection and all is well.

31. DR. SYNTAX TAKING POSSESSION OF HIS LIVING.

After a few days, Squire Worthy's letter arrives offering Syntax a position as Vicar in a Lake District town and as private tutor to his son for the handsome sum of £400 a year. After a stop at Oxford to visit his old friend Dicky Bend, the Doctor, his wife, his stableman Ralph and old Grizzle make their grand entrance into their new home in Sommerden:

>The courteous people lin'd the way,
>And their rude, untaught homage pay;
>The foremost of the assembled crowd,
>The fat Exciseman, humbly bow'd.
>"Welcome," he said, "to Sommerden!"
>The Clerk stood by and cry'd, "Amen!"
>Grizzle dash'd boldly through the gate,
>Where the kind Squire and Ladies wait,
>With kind embrace, with heart and hand,
>To cheer them into Cumberland.
>The bells rang loud, the boys huzza'd:
>The bonfire was in order laid;
>The villagers their zeal display,
>And ale and crackers close the day.

II

THE SECOND TOUR
OF DOCTOR SYNTAX,
IN SEARCH OF CONSOLATION

32. DR. SYNTAX AND HIS COUNTERPART.

In early editions, prior to the combining of the three tours, this drawing served as a frontispiece, in spite of the fact that the scene it depicts occurs half-way through Book II. It was likely that this illustration was featured to attract the reader's interest and to avoid opening the volume with the drawings depicting a death and funeral. The drawing illustrates a scene in which Syntax meets a Curate who has agreed to explain the Skimmington Ceremony to Syntax and who also bears remarkable resemblance to the newly-acclaimed writer:

So like in ev'ry point of view	At length, all drolleries explain'd,
Of hat and wig and features too,	A friendly social humour reign'd.
It might be thought the artist's hand	The table smil'd with plenteous fare,
Did our original command . . .	The bottle and the bowl were there,
Th' invited Curate soon appear'd	And 'mid the pipe's ascending smoke
The Doctor rubb'd his eyes and star'd . . .	The counterparts alternate spoke.

33. DR. SYNTAX LAMENTING THE LOSS OF HIS WIFE.

In spite of his wife's demanding and domineering ways, their new life in the appealing
Lake District brought them sufficiently close to prompt the Doctor's genuine lament
over her death:

> And darling Dolly was no more.
> His agonising bosom burns,
> He raves, and stamps, and prays by turns:
> Grief made him wild, but not a tear
> Did on his pallid cheeks appear.
> Into the chair his form he threw,
> "Adieu," he said, "my Love, adieu!"
> The tears then came – the gushing flood
> Stream'd down his cheeks and did him good:
> They calm'd at least his furious mood.

34. DR. SYNTAX AT THE FUNERAL OF HIS WIFE.

With the added grief of mourning not only his wife's death in childbirth but also "a dead child that never liv'd", Syntax arrives at the village churchyard:

> Beside the yawning grave he stood,
> In fix'd and humble attitude,
> And with devotion's solemn air,
> Just whisper'd each appointed prayer;
> —When as the voice, with pious trust,
> Dealt out the dole of dust to dust,
> He gaz'd as Heaven were in his view,
> Then bent—and look'd a last adieu.

35. DOCTOR SYNTAX SETTING OUT
ON HIS SECOND TOUR.

In an attempt to console their grieving friend, the Worthy family urges him to set out on a second tour, this time in search of consolation. With his Irish stableman and travel companion Pat, Syntax takes off once again, this time on his new horse, Phillis, with Pat mounted with gentlemanly pride on his steed, Punch:

> Syntax, now with a solemn grace,
> Gave his best friends a warm embrace;
> When many a kind adieu return'd,
> The wish with which their bosoms burn'd,
> That ev'ry good which Heav'n could send him,
> That no misfortune should attend him,
> Each rustic bosom did prepare
> And utter'd, as a cordial prayer!
> Thus the good man, at early day,
> Proceeded on his destin'd way.

36. DR. SYNTAX AND THE GYPSIES.

After several days of riding, writing and sketching in the Lake District and holding lengthy conversations with an itinerate artist, Syntax and Pat come upon "a throng, a medley troop" of gypsies, one of whom Pat discovers is an old military mate. In this delightful drawing, Pat is having his fortune told by two gypsy maidens, while a third one checks out his saddlebag. Around the fire with its marvellous gathering of characters, Syntax holds forth with a spirited lecture and takes the opportunity to conduct some oral history research on the origins and lore of the travelling band:

> Then leaving Phillis to the care
> Of wond'ring Pat, with solemn air
> He walk'd to view the motley band,
> And thus address'd them, while his hand
> Wav'd as a signal of command.
> They seem'd to give attentive ear
> His unexpected words to hear.

37. DOCTOR SYNTAX LOSES HIS WIG.

Shortly after retiring to a roadside inn, Syntax mistakes a bunch of rats for a "troop of cats" frolicking on his bedroom floor:

> He hiss'd and hooted, though in vain;
> They fled, but soon return'd again.
> To drive away this daring crew,
> He, with great force, his pillow threw . . .
> The shoes soon follow'd one another.
> The night-cap, too, now left his head;
> In vain the missle weapon fled . . .
> The rats, it seems, had play'd the rig
> In tearing up the Doctor's wig!

38. THE VISIT OF DR. SYNTAX TO THE WIDOW HOPEFULL AT YORK.

Taking off with his new wig, the traveller in search of consolation is set up by Squire and Madame Hearty at York to meet the Widow Hopefull:

> Syntax inspir'd and all alive,
> With humble air, that look'd like shame,
> Appear'd before th' expecting dame.
> But while she did the forms prepare
> Of who sits here, or who sits there,
> The Squire had popp'd behind the screen,
> To hear what pass'd and not be seen.

39. DR. SYNTAX AMUSED WITH PAT IN THE POND.

After several interesting adventures involving the Widow Hopefull and her friends, Squire and Madam Hearty, and Pat's brief encounter with the Maid Lucy, the two travellers move on. In the next adventure, Syntax leaves his steak and ale at an inn to find that Pat has jumped into the adjacent pond to escape a swarm of attacking bugs.

> Some noise, he knew not wherefore, broke
> Upon his rest, and straight he woke;
> When as he listen'd, it appear'd,
> That Pat's noisy language heard,
> And vulgar mirth seem'd to resound
> About the purlieus of a pond,
> Where Pat, up to his neck in water,
> Prov'd the droll cause of all the laughter.
> He op'd the casement and look'd out
> To see what Patrick was about.

40. DR. SYNTAX IN THE GLASS HOUSE.

This drawing suggests that Rowlandson's primary interest was to satirise popular tourist books rather than the picturesque. The commercial setting is an unusual subject for the artist. On their way from York to Eaton Hall, Syntax and Pat visit a glass making factory in Warrington, Lancashire, where they try out the blowers while other visitors cheer them on:

> Syntax now wish'd to try his skill
> In forming some neat utensil;
> When ev'ry part was duly fitted,
> And to his hand the tube submitted;
> The strict directions he obey'd,
> And something like a bottle made.
> Patrick too was prepar'd to blow
> A shape, tho' what he did not know.

41. DR. SYNTAX VISITS EATON HALL, CHESHIRE.

In Cheshire, the Doctor visits the great house, Eaton Hall, the ancestral home of the Grosvenor family. It is described by Combe in some detail, including the massive Gothic entrance hall with its display of chivalric armour and paintings:

> The morrow came, the city view'd,
> To Eaton they their way pursued,
> Where the Sage trac'd with prying eye
> The architect'ral pageantry.
> That taste and skill and labour'd art
> Had work'd and wrought in ev'ry part.

42. DR. SYNTAX MAKING HIS WILL.

On to Ludlow, where Syntax rhapsodises on the great English writers inspired by the castle. He falls asleep on the damp lawn and becomes ill. A physician is called, followed by a lawyer to assist him in making out his will:

> The Attorney came, a figure grave,
> And Syntax his instructions gave.
> As the period is uncertain
> When death may draw the sable curtain
> That shuts our man from all the strife,
> The joys, or casualties of life;
> He has a duty to fulfil,
> A solemn one, to make a will.

This drawing is aptly paired with Plate 43, as in both Rowlandson pokes fun at doctors and lawyers.

43. DR. SYNTAX IN A COURT OF JUSTICE.

As the travelling pair arrives in Bath, Pat is unexpectedly confronted by his former wife who, assuming that he had been killed in battle, has remarried, in the same way as she had married Pat, her second husband, following her first marriage to a wandering seafarer. The drawing, anticipating modern soap operas, comically depicts the court scene in which Syntax, at Pat's request, is seated next to the Mayor:

> A chairman came, a bustle rose,
> To angry words succeeded blows:
> And now the officers of peace
> Appear'd to make the riot cease,
> And force the parties to repair
> With their complaints before the Mayor.
> The Mayor, in chair of office seated
> Desir'd the grievance might be stated.
> When Patrick begg'd that he might send
> For Doctor Syntax to attend.

44. DR. SYNTAX PRESENT AT A COFFEE-HOUSE QUARREL AT BATH.

Combe's lines for this drawing speak for themselves in describing the coffee house argument with Syntax resolved to interpose as "Minister of Peace":

> Then sought the Coffee House to see
> The papers, and to take his tea.
> But it appear'd his fate to-day
> To be encounter'd with a fray:
> So far from finding social quiet,
> The room itself was in a riot:
> The angry mistress at the bar
> Was striving to appease the war;
> The waiter on the floor was thrown,
> And heaps of crock'ry tumbled down:
> Voices spoke loud, while tables rattle,
> With all the symbols of a battle.

45. DR. SYNTAX AND THE SUPERANNUATED FOX-HUNTER.

Syntax takes shelter from a storm in Nimrod Hall, the old abode of a "gouty Squire" who reminisces about his better days of hunting before he overdid his Port-wine "libations of the night", leading to his present life of decadence with equally antiquated hounds:

> With some good neighbours, sportsmen all,
> Who had just sought the shelt'ring hall,
> Dinner was serv'd, each took his place,
> And a View Halloo was the grace;
> But soon the Doctor did retire
> From noisy table to the fire.

46. DR. SYNTAX WITH THE SKIMMINGTON RIDERS.

Syntax is introduced to a jovial ceremony called 'Skimmington' in which a procession takes place to celebrate the triumph of an overbearing wife over a submissive and humbled husband. Rowlandson probably picked up this theme from a design by Hogarth for Butler's *Hudibras*, a satirical poem on Puritan hypocrisy. Combe's text describes some of the symbolism:

> Thus as he spoke the noisy throng,
> In due disorder pass'd along.
> With antlers which had whilom grac'd
> A stag's bold brow, on pitch-forks plac'd,
> The roaring, dancing bumpkins show,
> And the white smickets wave below,
> While suited to the rustic manners,
> The petticoats appear'd as banners.

47. DOCTOR SYNTAX & THE BEES.

While a guest of Lady Bounty at her stately home, Dr. Syntax is attacked by a swarm of bees, enabling Rowlandson to draw a scene of great visual comedy:

> When Lady Bounty to beguile
> His labours with approving smile,
> Stood on the terrace wall to view
> The Doctor's progress as he drew:
> When, at once furious and alarm'd,
> And, with most uncouth weapons arm'd,
> Led on by Pat, a noisy crew
> Did a wild swarm of bees pursue . . .
> But all their sounds were made in vain;
> They did their humming flight maintain,
> And spite of pan and pot and kettle,
> Chose on the Doctor's head to settle.

48. DR. SYNTAX VISITS A BOARDING SCHOOL
FOR YOUNG LADIES.

Lady Bounty takes the Doctor to her seminary for young women, where Syntax
lectures to them with advice on the history of gender differences and roles:

> The evening came, the scene was gay,
> All clad in summer's best array,
> When the fair youthful band were seen
> Arrang'd upon the shaven green.
> Beneath an oak's wide-spreading shade,
> While through its boughs the zephyr play'd,
> The sage with reverential pride,
> Plac'd the preceptress by his side . . .
> Then upward look'd, as if was given,
> A silent orison to Heaven;
> And soon a mute attention hung
> Upon the wisdom of his tongue.

49. DR. SYNTAX MAKING A DISCOVERY.

While sketching a sylvan scene by a crystal stream and parish church, the distracted artist comes upon Pat with Susan, a village maiden:

> Thus, passing on, he chanced to see,
> Beneath an overshadowing tree,
> Patrick engag'd in am'rous guise
> Devouring Susan with his eyes.

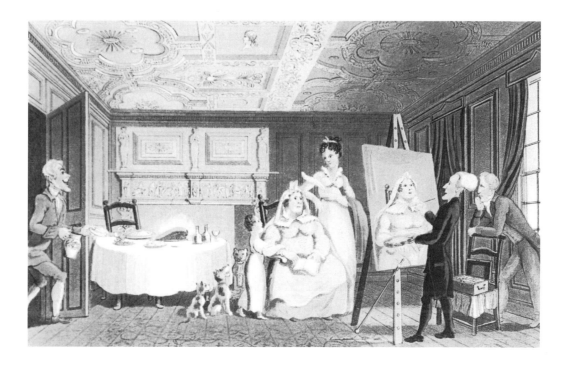

50. DR. SYNTAX PAINTING A PORTRAIT.

Before moving on from Bounty Hall, Syntax decides to favour his hostess by trying his hand at portraiture:

> He wav'd his pencil, form'd the line
> The shapes the human face divine,
> Gave all the features their due places,
> And hop'd to finish with the graces.
> Puffing painting, on he went,
> Sometimes displeas'd, sometimes content.
> The work, 'tis true, had no pretence
> To that superior excellence
> Which some could to the canvas give,
> Whereon the figures seem to live.

51. MARRIAGE OF DOCTOR DICKY BEND.

On to visit his old friend, Dicky Bend, Syntax does the honours at Bend's wedding:

> And Syntax here perform'd the rite
> Which did his worthy friend unite,
> In the indissoluble tie
> Which hallow'd altars sanctify.

52. DOCTOR SYNTAX AT AN AUCTION.

This print and Plate 53 make an interesting commentary on authors, publishers and booksellers in London at that time. Syntax, having arrived in London, muses on the public reception of his first book. He comes upon an auction with books selling at good prices. When his own book comes up for bids, his sketching talent is compared to that of Rowlandson:

> Its value was most warmly stated,
> Its Author's talents celebrated,
> Its humour, verse, and moral powers
> Suited to grave and laughing hours,
> And deck'd by nature and by fun,
> With the gay skill of ROWLANDSON.
> Syntax, delighted beyond measure,
> Nodded to express his pleasure,
> But started when the auctioneer
> Told him he was the purchaser.

Objecting that his approving nod was taken as a two-pound bid for his own book, Syntax is now recognised as the author. He, therefore, autographs his volume and it goes up again to sell for nearly double, much to his glee.

53. DR. SYNTAX AND THE BOOKSELLER.

Following his successful sale, Syntax is now warmly welcomed by Vellum, the printer-publisher introduced in the First Tour:

> Vellum who was waiting there
> Came in for his allotted share:
> He had the auction story heard,
> And brought his hopes to be preferr'd,
> As printer, publisher, what not,
> By which some profits might be got,
> If Syntax had to London brought
> Any new work by fancy taught,
> Which might his character maintain
> And promise a return of gain.

54. DR. SYNTAX AT FREEMASON'S HALL.

His fame now spreading, Syntax is invited by a book-worm, Knight the Sage, to see his book collection and to address the company at Freemasons' Hall. The author-cleric chooses as his topic the genius of native talent and his modest hope that his own contribution as "Artist and Christian Priest" will hasten the day when "British Arts may rival Greece".

> The day soon came when Bookworm's call
> Summon'd him to Freemasons' Hall.
> A num'rous company appear'd,
> The several toasts were loudly cheer'd;
> And after he had calmly heard
> Displays of various eloquence,
> Replete with warm and manly sense,
> From royal lips with noble mind;
> In gen'ral praises Syntax join'd:
> At length he felt his bosom fir'd,
> And with the love of art inspir'd,
> He rose, his modest silence broke;
> And thus the zealous Doctor spoke.

55. MISS WORTHY'S MARRIAGE:
DR. SYNTAX IN THE CHAIR.

Back to Worthy Hall on a lake shore in Cumberland, Syntax does the honours at Miss
Worthy's marriage, thus bringing his Second Tour to a close. However, concluding
with a wedding ceremony for the daughter of a valued family leaves the door open
for a Third Tour, already in progress, in which Doctor Syntax will travel in search of
a wife.

> And as the plenteous feast began,
> The board was crown'd, the vessels ran,
> From whence the foaming cups o'erflow'd;
> And ev'ry beast with pleasure glow'd.
> The happy Syntax took the chair,
> Beside him were the wedded pair,
> While near him all in smiling state
> The Squire and His Maria sate,
> Who never had such pleasure known
> Since such a day had been their own.

III

THE THIRD TOUR
OF DOCTOR SYNTAX,
IN SEARCH OF A WIFE

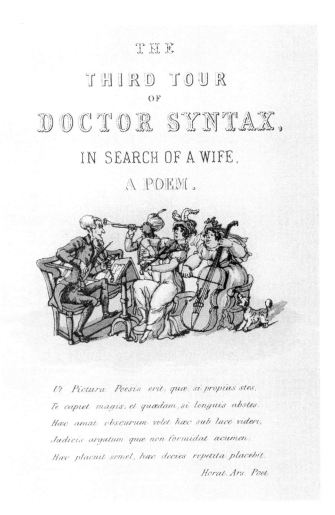

56. TITLE PAGE. *THE THIRD TOUR OF DOCTOR SYNTAX, IN SEARCH OF A WIFE.*

The title page for the Third Tour features an amusing musical ensemble as a preview to one of the scenes to follow (Plate 67) in which Syntax is invited to share one of his several talents. The inscription is from Horace's *Art of Poetry* and reads:

> Poetry is like painting: one piece takes your fancy if you stand close to it, another
> if you keep some distance. One courts a dim light, another, challenging keen crit-
> icism, will fain be seen in the glare; this charms but once, that will please ten
> times repeated.

Those who make it through the Latin will have the added pleasure of speculating on the inscription's application to the poetry and paintings of Doctor Syntax's Third Tour, in which he is in search of a wife.

57. DOCTOR SYNTAX SETTING OUT IN SEARCH OF A WIFE.

Lonely now without his wife, Syntax sets out once again, this time with a marital mission:

> On the morn his breakfast done,
> With not a cloud to hide the sun,
> The Doctor did his way pursue,
> And, in a trotting hour or two
> Bumpkin's old hall appear'd in view,
> When soon he saw his hearty host
> Leaning most idly 'gainst a post . . .
> And when he their approach espied,
> Bill Bumpkin clapp'd his hands and cried,
> "My worthy Parson, is it you?"

58. DOCTOR SYNTAX SOLILOQUISING.

Reflecting in silence on his loneliness, Syntax is offered advice from Old Marg'ret, the village "sage gran'nam". She encourages him to move on in his matrimonial quest:

> The dame had pass'd her early day
> In service to the great and gay;
> And was well-pleas'd to have it known
> What stations she had held in town;
> Would gravely boast where she had been,
> And tell the fine things she had seen:
> In short, at threescore years of age,
> She was become a rural sage.

59. DOCTOR SYNTAX TURNED NURSE.

Having been invited by the enthusiastic equestrian, Squire Bill Bumpkin and his wife to join them at Bumpkin Manor in Westmoreland, Syntax offers them some marriage counseling. Madam Bumpkin, in turn, suggests that Syntax call on her botanist friend, the Widow Hyacinth, as a possible marriage prospect (the first of several to be recommended to the searching suitor). Moving on, Syntax and Pat take refuge from a storm at the cottage of Farmer John Good and his wife, Mary, where he demonstrates his paternal instincts with their brood.

It is not needful to relate
"I see one great command obey'd:
With that you piously comply:
I mean, INCREASE AND MULTIPLY."
Himself and the good dame to please,
He took the children on his knees;
The danced the urchins to and fro,
And sung as nurses often do.

60. THE BANNS FORBIDDEN.

After lengthy advice on marriages and re-marriages from such characters as Sir Stately at Stirrup Hall, Squire Ned Easy and his wife Kate, and the bachelor Bob Single, Syntax plots his courtship with several suggested prospects, including Miss Crotchet at Tulip Hall. His Quest is momentarily delayed, however, when he meets the aged and wealthy Widow Horner.

> One morning as in the churchyard walking
> And to himself was calmly talking;
> While Mat, the Sexton, sung a stave,
> Half in and half out of a grave:
> He was saluted by a dame,
> And Cath'rine Horner was her name.

Widow Horner's young intended, Jack, is quite willing to wed the nag to inherit her fortune. Syntax promptly declines their request for his ceremonial services by forbidding the banns. The Sexton holds the skull of the widow's deceased husband, reminds her of her "wanton sin", chases away young Jack, and pelts the widow with her late husband's bones.

61. DOCTOR SYNTAX WITH A BLUE-STOCKING BEAUTY.

Now riding on Punch, his valet's former nag (which will take centre stage in a later drawing) Syntax sets his sights on marrying a wealthy but younger and more beautiful "Widow Horner". He travels to the "embower'd spot" presided over by the witty blue-stocking beauty, the Widow Omicron, recommended to him by Sir Stately of Stirrup Hall. She praises his wit, feeds and flatters him and debates ideas of love. It nearly exhausts him. No wonder that:

> In this fair lady are combin'd
> The beauties of the form and mind;
> Is rich withal, and has withstood
> Five years of tempting widowhood,
> When many a suitor, but in vain,
> Has strove her favour to obtain. . .
> She plac'd him in a satin chair,
> 'Tween Mercury and Jupiter,
> And plac'd a stool with fruitage drest,
> One which his either foot to rest.

62. THE CELLAR QUARTETTO.

On the way to Tulip Hall and the prospects of courting Miss Crochet, Syntax meets the Physician, Dr. Julep. Together they visit the Lawyer, Capias, whose overindulgence in wine and ale require the Physician's continual and well-paid services. In the cellar vaults with "ever-moving" glasses of libation in their "Bacchanalian Feast", they form an intoxicated trio representing Medicine, Law and Divinity. Rebecca, the household maid, is pursuaded to join them, thus becoming the fourth member of the 'Cellar Quartetto'. Syntax's amourous interest is plain:

> Attended by a household dame
> Whom we shall now Rebecca name.
> Thither he dragg'd his wooded chair
> And took a fix'd position there:
> To Becky's hand he gave a squeeze,
> And thus addressed her, "If you please
> I'll taste your tempting toasted cheese."
> "No Sir," she said, "Here's better picking,
> Broil'd ham and a nice mushroom chicken."

63. DOCTOR SYNTAX PRESENTING A FLORAL OFFERING.

Finally arriving at the "balmy sweets" of the "blooming mansion" of Tulip Hall, the courting cleric presents a floral calling card to "a damsel full of joke and laughter" in the window of the nearby parson's vicarage. Her father gone to a church meeting, she accepts his gift and his hopes to call again:

He did his fragrant gift present,
She revell'd in the charming scent,
And smil'd a grateful compliment.
A matron who was on the watch,
From upper window in the thatch,
Thought it but proper to descend,
And give the warnings of a friend.
"I'm sister, Sir, to our Divine,
Nay, that Miss, is a niece of mine,
And much I wish to hint to you,
What my good brother's self would do;
That you must your keen thoughts prepare
To guard against some hidden snare,
By which you may become the tool
Of Lady Tulip's ridicule."

64. THE BILLIARD TABLE.

The young beauties of Tulip Hall welcome Syntax, join him in dinner and invite him
to their billiard table:

> At length the temple of perfume
> Was quitted for the billiard room.
> Ladies command, he must obey,
> So Syntax too a Cue to play,
> Tho' he did not the laugh approve
> As he proposed to play for love,
> Or when the usual sum was nam'd,
> For which these ladies always gam'd.
> But, yet it seem'd as if he won,
> Though when the pastime they had done,
> He was inform'd, and to his cost,
> The several parties he had lost . . .
> So he put on a smiling face,
> And paid his losings with a grace.

65. MISFORTUNE AT TULIP HALL.

The next morning, Ma'am Tulip guides Syntax to her famed Tulip Conservatory, where he is obviously out of place:

> Careful, and step by step, he mov'd,
> But just as he successful prov'd
> A shelf gave way, another follow'd,
> Ma'am Tulip scream'd, the gard'ner halloo'd,
> While Syntax join'd the gen'ral bawling,
> And soon upon the ground was sprawling;
> When, scatter'd round upon the green,
> Pots, flowers, and hat and wig were seen.

66. THE HARVEST HOME.

On his way to Crotchet Lodge, the home of the Widow Crotchet, Syntax and Pat hear distant shouts of joy, and a rural peasant parade approaches:

At length Pat cried, "I see them come,
And faith, it is a harvest home."
Said Syntax, "What a charm to see
this show of glad simplicity!" . . .
The throng'd procession now drew near,
In front the mingled groups appear
Of joyful peasants who employ
Their voices loud, in hymns of joy.
Then came the lab'ring waggon's load,

Dragg'd on along the winding road,
Rich with the sheaves the harvest yields,
The closing bounty of the fields . . .
Syntax would now his skill display
Among the minstrels of the day,
And ask'd a fiddle to be sought;
The instrument was quickly brought;
It answer'd to his active hand,
When he march'd and led the band.

67. THE GARDEN TRIO.

This drawing depicts a scene suggested on the title page of the Third Tour and shares with Plate 66 a musical theme. Miss Crochet invites Syntax to share his fiddling talents by joining her "little School of Harmony".

> At length came the appointed hour
> When, in the garden's gaudy bower,
> Where flowers and climbing plants o'erlaid,
> Combin'd to form a scented shade,
> These vot'ries of sweet sounds appear
> To wake Apollo's list'ning ear.
> Miss C_____ began with furious force,
> The Doctor follow'd her of course,
> While the old Dame with slower pace
> Came rumbling after on the bass.

68. DOCTOR SYNTAX AT A CARD PARTY.

Syntax's next visit is to Comet Place, the residence of the "fair astronomer", Lady Macnight, who feeds him a delightful meal and invites him to test his skills at her card party:

> Meal done, the patronising dame
> Propos'd some lively gen'ral game;
> And Syntax drew his ready chair
> In the night's play to take a share.

69. DOCTOR SYNTAX STAR-GAZING.

Lady Macnight next leads Syntax to her rooftop observatory, while Pat, with his mind on less celestial matters, steals the show:

> The meal by frequent signals sought,
> Pat now in eager hurry brought;
> But whether 'twas the slipp'ry floor,
> Or running dog, or banging door,
> It may not be required to tell;
> Certain it is the valet fell,
> Swore a loud oath, when plate and platter
> And spoons and sauce-boats made a clatter;
> While yelping curs, or kick'd or wounded,
> Were in the gen'ral din confounded . . .
> Pat's feet gave way, his balance lost,
> His paunch to right and left was tost.

After extended debate with Lady Macnight on the planets and gender, Syntax realises that the two of them could never overcome their differences on astronomy. She suggests that he visit Mrs. Brisket, who shares his views, and offers to set him up with an artist friend, Miss Pallet, with whom he would have even more in common.

70. DR. SYNTAX IN THE WRONG LODGING HOUSE.

Resolved either to find a wife in London or to return home, Syntax stops by Pater-
noster Row to visit his bookseller friend, Vellum, who is amused to learn that Syntax
has mistakenly taken a room in a "snughouse in Mary-bonne", a "house of ill-fame".
Although Syntax has demonstrated throughout his tours his attraction to the ladies,
this is the closest that he comes to an illicit affair. Therefore, the moralistic Combe has
Pat handle the situation.

And Syntax sought his novel home.
To the opening door there came
The old, fat, grinning, prating dame,
Who begg'd that he would take a chair
In her boudoir, and seat him there:
Smart, well-dress'd, giggling Misses three,
Compos'd the old lady's company . . .
He was next morn in full array

And planning out the future day,
When Pat appear'd quite pale and wan,
And thus in ruffled tones began.
"I hope you will not take offence
If I just tell your Reverence,
This is a house of evil-fame.
I know its character and name!"

71. DR. SYNTAX RECEIVED BY THE MAID
INSTEAD OF THE MISTRESS.

After settling a deal with Vellum to publish a volume of his sermons, Syntax sends an introductory note to Mrs. Brisket who, in turn, invites him to visit. The vivacious lady, enjoying a good joke, instructs Molly, the maid, to greet him as the mistress of the house, leaving the embarrassed Syntax to look elsewhere for a less mischievous spouse.

All in due time a stout housemaid
Was like the lady's self array'd;
The pendants dangle from her ears,
The plumage o'er her brow appears;
The ostrich spoils so green and red,
Bent graceful from her auburn head . . .
But Molly in this tonish dress
Was the sublime of awkwardness . . .

As Syntax, by the trick betray'd
Would for the Mistress take the Maid,
And let forth many a classic speech
Which pedant gallantry might teach;
While Madam, from some cushion'd height,
Not seen, nor yet quite out of sight,
Could from behind a curtain's sweep
With silent caution take a peep.

72. THE ARTIST'S ROOM.

Syntax's next visit is to the artist, Miss Pallet, who invites him to dinner to meet her two artist friends who delight in running down all other artists of the day. Syntax uses his own sketching pencil to let his hostess and her friends know what he thinks:

> Thus, having clos'd their critic law,
> They Syntax ask'd if he could draw:
> When he his ready pencil took
> And in the blank page of a book
> Design'd a gallows from which swung
> Two figures that by cordage hung.
> "Pray," it was said, "who may be those?
> They are two murderers, I suppose."
> "Yes," Syntax said, "of my formation,
> They're murderers of REPUTATION!"

73. THE DEATH OF PUNCH.

The next problem facing Syntax is the death of the horse he has shared with Pat during the second tour. Syntax tries to console his valet-stableman and asks Glanders, the veterinarian, how the horse died:

> "Now Pat, I pray you hold your peace,"
> The Doctor said, "your wailing cease:
> I'm sorry that I've lost the mare,
> But 'tis a loss which we can bear."
> Syntax spoke, when Glanders there
> Was looking at the breathless mare;
> "What caus'd her death, Sir?" ask'd the sage.
> "Hard work," old Glanders said, "and age."

74. THE ADVERTISEMENT FOR A WIFE.

A letter from Mrs. Brisket informs Syntax of her matchmaking efforts in advertising for a wife for him. Her efforts pay off amazingly well, and he is overwhelmed by a delegation of mothers, aunts, guardians and others, all bringing their blushing would-be brides to demonstrate their love. Fortunately, Pat is enthusiastically prepared to assist his Sire:

> "Ladies," he said, "I plainly see
> The tricks that you would play with me.
> In all that's said, in all that's done,
> I see 'tis Mistress Brisket's fun;
> I feel I am a very fool
> And well deserve your ridicule:
> But if you do not quickly go,
> A constable the way shall show."
> Says Pat, "I hear, Sir, your commands.
> I'll take the ladies off your hands!
> I'll do your ladyships no harm;
> I'll kiss you well and make you warm."

75. DR. SYNTAX AND THE FOUNDLING.

Still without a wife, Syntax becomes an instant father when he discovers an abandoned baby boy left on his doorstep. This may have been an inclusion by Combe to keep the door open for possible sequels, given the great success of the first two books. In fact, the foundling did appear less than a year after the publication of the Third Tour in the Combe-Rowlandson series *Johnny Quæ Genus, or The Little Foundling*.

> He op'd the door, and 'gan to stare,
> For lo, no visitor was there:
> But, looking onward to the floor,
> There was a basket cover'd o'er
> With a warm blanket, which, remov'd,
> The covering of an infant proved:
> There a sweet, lovely baby slept
> And look'd as if it ne'er had wept . . .
> He told the laundress to apply
> To the parochial ministry
> That ev'ry sacred rite be done,
> And the poor child be christen'd John.

76. THE RESULT OF PURCHASING A BLIND HORSE.

After Punch's demise, Syntax sets out to buy another mount. At an auction, he bids, pays his money and rides off in equestrian pride, not realising that his new purchase could not see:

> But she set off at such a rate
> That, as she pass'd the turn-pike gate,
> The toll-man well nigh met his fate.
> Away the hat and peruke flew,
> A cabbage-merchant he o'erthrew;
> And while she in the highway lay'd,
> Her angry donkey kick'd and bray'd;
> Nay, nought could check the wild mare's rage
> But running headlong 'gainst a stage!

77. A NOBLE HUNTING PARTY.

After getting a new horse from his London friend, Sir John, Syntax is grateful for a steed that outdoes Old Grizzle and Punch. He also realises that he must move on, having "gain'd no wife, but found a child". Before departing, however, Syntax is invited by Sir John to join him and his noble party in a fox hunt so he could try out his new horse and demonstrate his equestrian skills—not among Syntax's highest accomplishments:

> Swift as the wind my Lady went:
> She was the Dian of the day,
> O'er hill and dale she brush'd away,
> And left the Doctor to pursue
> The pack, which never caught his view.
> But whether that he could not keep
> His saddle as he took a leap,
> Or by what strange mischance he fell,
> He could not, or he would not tell:
> Between two banks he was seen sprawling,
> And, loud enough, for mercy calling.

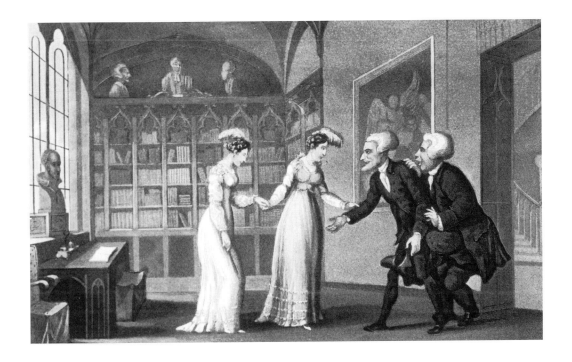

78. INTRODUCTION TO COURTSHIP.

On his way back to his home, Syntax revisits his old friend, Dicky Bend, who urges him to meet a family friend who "has enough of what is good to fill your void of widowhood".

> The following day, the lady came;
> Nor need I tell her maiden name,
> For ere a week or so was o're
> That maiden name was her's no more.
> On the third day, kind Mrs. Bend,
> Who with both, as mutual friend,
> Had talk'd the important matter over,
> Presented Syntax as a Lover;
> While Dicky whisper'd, "Push it well,
> And you'll soon bear away the belle . . .
> And she said AY, within the hour,
> Nay, on the third or fourth day after,
> They were both noos'd in Hymen's garter.

79. DR. SYNTAX IN DANGER.

After two years of happy marriage and raising the young foundling, Dr. Syntax becomes a new man, "so nicely dress'd and always clean, he might be taken for a Dean." The Doctor and his Mistress of the Rectory become well beloved of the parish and of Syntax's old friends, the Worthy's. However, Syntax becomes gravely ill after plunging into a lake to save his wife from drowning.

> The Doctor in a hurry came,
> And found the system in a flame.
> The lancet to profusion bled,
> The blisters cover'd back and head,
> And Syntax was convey'd to bed.
> When there reclin'd, his upward eye
> Seem'd as commercing with the sky,
> And his hand wav'd, as if to tell,
> This is a long and last farewell!
> Torpor then o'er his senses crept,
> And he appear'd as if he slept:
> But Death had given the final stroke;
> For from that sleep he ne're awoke.

80. THE FUNERAL OF DR. SYNTAX.

O 'twas a melancholy scene
When he was borne along the green!
What train of mourners did appear,
And scarce an eye without a tear . . .
The village wept. The hamlets round
Crowded the consecrated ground
And waited there to see the end
Of Pastor, Teacher, Father, Friend!

And Combe adds his own final word:

My verse has now no more to tell.
The story's done. SYNTAX, FAREWELL!

CHAPTER THREE

THE EXTENDED SYNTAX FAMILY
IN THE NINETEENTH CENTURY

EVEN AS ROWLANDSON PUT HIS FINAL STROKES ON HIS DRAWING OF 'THE Funeral of Doctor Syntax' (Plate 80) and Combe penned an obituary verse for the deceased cleric, it was increasingly obvious to the ambitious Ackermann and his talented collaborators that their creation had taken on a extended life among a growing number of Syntax fans. In addition to the numerous British editions and reissuings of the First Tour between 1812 and 1820 and the publication of the Third Tour in late 1820, the First Tour was published, without illustrations, in Copenhagen in 1820, in 1821 a French edition appeared with plates based on Rowlandson's, and a German edition was published in Berlin in 1822.[1]

Shortly after the late 1820 publication of the Third Tour and the early 1821 publication of the combined trilogy, Ackermann commissioned Rowlandson and Combe to produce a Syntax sequel. No doubt the decision was sparked not only by the popularity of the various translations but also by a rash of imitations appearing between 1815 and 1821, using the Syntax name either in the title or as the author's pseudonym. Several of these imitations will be discussed later. For the moment, however, it is sufficient to note that Combe, in the preface to the third edition of the Second Tour in 1820, found it necessary to write:

> It has been the opinion of many whose superior judgement commanded my submission, that I was called upon to separate the work written by me as the biographer of "Doctor Syntax" from those which have been palmed upon the public by others who have pilfered that title. This book, the *First Tour of Doctor Syntax in Search of the Picturesque*, the *Dance of Death* and the *Dance of Life*, are the only works, in this style of composition, which have been written by me.

Given the obvious recognition of such pilferings, even if, at best, they were signs of the merits and popularity of the original work, it is little wonder that Ackermann was prepared to produce another work using the successful Combe-Rowlandson team. It was therefore perhaps intentional that at the end of the Third Tour, Syntax inherits the foundling (Plate 75), christens him John, and leaves him in the care of his widowed second wife. At any rate, just three months after Rowlandson had completed the trilogy with 'The Funeral of Doctor Syntax', the first plates were published launching the sequel, *The History of Johnny Quæ Genus, the Little Foundling of the Late Doctor Syntax*, appearing in eight parts, five in 1821 and three in 1822. This was to be the last work by Combe, published just months before his death in 1823. Perhaps Combe himself recognised that his failing health was weakening his writing and the active imagination that had sustained the Syntax character. Clearly, the verses are much poorer and the Johnny Quæ Genus character much less developed. Combe's prefatory comments suggest both his intentions and limitations:

> The favour which has been bestowed on the different tours of Doctor Syntax, has encouraged the Writer of them to give a History of the Foundling, who has been thought an interesting Object in the latter of those volumes; and it is written in the same style and manner, with a view to connect them.
>
> This Child of Chance, it is presumed, is led through a track of Life not unsuited to the peculiarity of his Condition and Character, while its varieties, as in the former works, are represented by the pencil of MR. ROWLANDSON with its accustomed characteristic felicity.
>
> The idea of an English Gil Blas predominated through the whole of this volume; which must be considered as fortunate in no common degree, if its readers, in the course of their perusal, should be disposed to acknowledge even a remote similitude to the incomparable work of LA SAGE.
>
> It may, perhaps, be considered as presumption in me, and at my age, to sport even with my own Dowdy Muse, but, from the extensive patronage which DOCTOR SYNTAX has received, it may be presumed that, more or less, he has continued to amuse. And I, surely, have no reason to be dissatisfied, when Time points at my eightieth Year, that I can still afford some pleasure to those who are disposed to be pleased.[2]

Although *Johnny Quæ Genus* does not match up to the Tours of Doctor Syntax, it does contain however twenty-four coloured illustrations by Rowlandson which may interest collectors. Therefore, I have provided a brief commentary from the book. A complete set of the illustrations is reproduced in Appendix 2.

The book begins with an explanation of Johnny's odd name, given to him by Syntax—after a few cups of wine with Squire Worthy, Syntax had decided on a classical "name which none e'er had before". Syntax's old friend, Dickey Bend, pledges to look after the boy's education, and another Syntax character, the bookseller Vellum, also reappears in the sequel. After the death of Mrs. Syntax, the slightly humped-back young man sets off for a journey to London (no. 1). While in London, he seeks his fortune as a talented lackey with extraordinary talents for flattery. He gains employment with a variety of characters such as the wealthy Sir

Jeff'ry Gourmand, with whose servant he discovers pleasant pastimes (no. 8); the quack physician Anodyne; several wealthy widows; the eccentric portrait painter, Mr. Carmine; and an assortment of gamblers and money-lenders who play on his talents, tenacity and tendency for trouble.

Johnny receives several visitations from the ghost of his adoptive father who admonishes him to make amends for his sins and errors and recommends a life of an honest gentleman. Johnny takes the name of Squire Free-born and tries to play the role, but is soon confronted by his creditors. At this point, the old bookseller Vellum and the now aged laundress Betty Broom reappear and identify him as the son and heir of Vellum's old friend, the prominent and honoured but dying Lawyer Fairman. Vellum and Betty bring him to Fairman (no. 24) whose final act in life is to bless his new found son. After a few years of reformed life as a country squire, Quæ Genus goes to an early grave, still attended by old Vellum and Betty Broom.

The History of Johnny Quæ Genus was not as popular as the Syntax Tours, though it benefited from the Syntax reputation and, perhaps especially, from the Rowlandson drawings. It was reissued throughout the nineteenth century and was published in New York by Appleton and Company as late as 1903.

Of less interest to Rowlandson collectors but still worth some attention here, are the large number of publications influenced by the Syntax Family that appeared during the early nineteenth century and later Victorian era, especially the numerous imitations noted earlier. In 1815, *The Life of Napoleon, a Hudibrastic Poem in Fifteen Cantos* was produced in London bearing the name Doctor Syntax as the author. Of special significance are the thirty engravings by George Cruik-shank, the prominent illustrator known later for his associations with Charles Dickens. Also, in 1815 in London, *The Adventures of Doctor Comicus, or the Frolicks of Fortune*, a book by 'A Modern Syntax', was published, claiming to be "a comical satirical poem for the squeamish and the queer" and possibly using the name "Comicus" as a play on Combe's name. In 1819, Doctor Syntax was declared as the author of a narrative poem, *The Wars of Wellington*. And so the list goes on.

Among several imitations of Combe's Syntax-style poetry were two books on the adventures of a travelling military officer whose antics somewhat resemble those of the Combe-Rowlandson creation, Johnny Quæ Genus. The first book, *The Military Adventures of Johnny Newcome, with an Account of his Campaigne on the Penninsula and the Pall Mall*, was published in London in 1816. Written anonymously "By an Officer" (identified as David Roberts), the book contains drawings by Rowlandson (such as fig. 4, 'Johnny Newcome Going to Lay in Stock') bearing some

Fig. 4. 'Johnny Newcome Going to Lay in Stock' by Thomas Rowlandson. From *The Military Adventures of Johnny Newcome* by 'an Officer' [David Roberts], London 1816.

resemblance to his later Johnny Quæ Genus. A second book, with a slightly changed spelling of the hero's name, was published three years later by John Mitford and entitled *The Adventures of Johnny Newcombe in the Navy* (London: Sherwood, Neely & Jones, 1819). Perhaps 'Newcombe' was a pun on Combe's name.

Three of these imitations enjoyed particular success, all of which are discussed by Anthony Gully. The first was *Sam Syntax's Description of the Cries of London as They Are Daily Exhibited in the Streets* by an unknown author and artist, which went into a second printing in 1821.[3] The second, also published in 1820, was a poem by 'Doctor Syntax' called *The Tour of Doctor Syntax Through London*. This contained some interesting illustrations, suggested by Gully as possibly being by Isaac Cruikshank while others have suggested that Rowlandson himself had a possible hand in the work (fig. 5). This book was a great success even though it lacked the unique humour of the original Syntax tours. In this story, Syntax and his wife are cast as London tourists whose unfamiliarity with city ways make them easy targets for hawkers and cheats.

The last of these, published by W. Wright in London also in 1820, was *Doctor Syntax in Paris, or a Tour in Search of the Grotesque* with illustrations by E. Williams. Three of the illustrations in *Doctor Syntax in Paris*—'Doctor Syntax Embarking at

Fig. 5. 'The Rev. Doctor Syntax and his Spouse' from *The Tour of Doctor Syntax Through London*, published in 1820 by J. Johnson of Cheapside, London. Illustrated by an unsigned artist imitating Rowlandson's Syntax character. Anthony Gully suggests that the artist may have been Isaac Cruikshank.

Dover' (fig. 6), 'Doctor Syntax Arrives at Paris' (fig. 7), and 'Doctor Syntax Conducted to the Prefecture on a Charge of Liberalism' (fig. 8)—suggest why some consider the Williams illustrations among the better Rowlandson imitations.

In 1821, Williams worked with W. Read on twenty plates for *The Tour of Doctor Prosody, In Search of the Antique and Picturesque, through Scotland, the Hebrides, the Orkney and Shetland Islands*. Prosody, probably a grammatical spoof on Syntax, travels with the deceitful Dr. Factobend and the loyal buffoon Archy. Prosody's success led to an imitation of an imitation, *The Adventures of the Reverend Doctor*

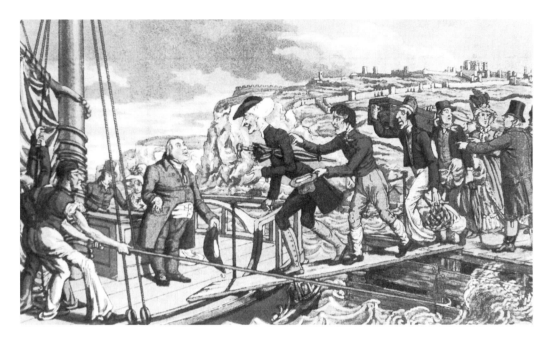

Fig. 6. 'Doctor Syntax embarking at Dover' by E. Williams. From *Doctor Syntax in Paris, or a Tour in Search of the Grotesque*, London 1820.

Fig. 7. 'Doctor Syntax Arrives at Paris' by E. Williams. From *Doctor Syntax in Paris, or a Tour in Search of the Grotesque*, London 1820.

Fig. 8. 'Doctor Syntax Conducted to the Prefecture on a Charge of Liberalism' by E. Williams. From *Doctor Syntax in Paris, or a Tour in Search of the Grotesque*, London 1820.

Prosody in the Island of Rathlin (1865) in which Syntax's descendant leaves for his tour on a train. As Gully notes, the numerous translations and imitations, many of which are set outside of the British Isles, suggest the widespread popularity of Syntax and his impostors and the interest of booksellers to reach an increasingly wide regional and foreign readership. It is also worth noting that Pierce Egan's popular *Tom and Jerry* adventure series illustrated by Isaac and George Cruikshank began with Jerry Hawthorn's and Corinthian Tom's "rambles and sprees" in *Life in London* in 1821 before moving on, Syntax-like, to France and Ireland.

Not all of the Doctor Syntax derivatives consisted of translations and imitations. Indeed, the Combe-Rowlandson Tours were published in new editions and reissuings by Ackermann and by others throughout the nineteenth century. These are listed in the next chapter, but a few are worth special mention here. First is the miniature edition of the *Three Tours* (3" x 6"), published in 1823, the year of Combe's death. After Rowlandson's death in 1827 and Ackermann's in 1834, the Ackermann firm published the *First Tour* with new illustrations by 'Alfred Crowquill' (Alfred Henry Forrester), later to become a prominent artist for *Punch*. Crowquill obviously remained faithful to Rowlandson's originals, as is evident in

left Fig. 9. Version of Doctor Syntax in his study by 'Alfred Crowquill' (Alfred Henry Forrester). From 1838 reissue of *Doctor Syntax in Search of the Picturesque*.

right Fig. 10. 'A flight of volumes in the air / In various bindings, gilt and fair.' Version of Doctor Syntax's dream of books by 'Alfred Crowquill' (Alfred Henry Forrester). From 1838 reissue of *Doctor Syntax in Search of the Picturesque*.

three examples: the frontispiece of Doctor Syntax in his study (fig. 9; compare to Plate 1) and Syntax in his dream of books (fig. 10; compare to Plate 29). A second noteworthy edition is one published in 1868 by Chatto & Windus containing John Camden Hotten's account of Combe's life, the first ever published.

As long as there was public interest in the Syntax cult, there were those ready to capitalise in attracting the customers. Gully documents several stage productions, such as an 1820 Christmas pantomime at the Adelphi Theatre; an 1821 musical extravaganza, *Doctor Syntax, or Harlequin in London*; another 'operatic farce' based on Doctor Syntax in London, produced at Sadler's Wells Theatre in 1823; and one by Charles Dibdin, *Dr. Syntax and Another Doctor*, produced in 1823 at the Davis Royal Amphitheatre.

The extent to which the Syntax Family expanded during the remaining decades of the nineteenth century is described by John Hotten in his 1868 biographical sketch of Combe:

> The good-natured, moralising Syntax at once became a public character and a general favourite. His distinctive portrait . . . and his singular features as drawn by Rowlandson were as unmistakable as his perpetual good-humour, in the midst

of troubles and mishaps, described by Combe. The creation was a success, and as Paul Pry gave a name to all sorts of objects ten years later, so Syntax was the popular title in his day.[4]

Hotten's reference is to Paul Pry, a character who, like Mr. Punch, was made famous by a popular illustrated magazine. Scores of copies later appeared in Britain, America and other countries as engraving and lithography techniques developed during the Victorian era, replacing the much slower engraving and aquatinting processes used in earlier book and magazine decoration. Even the name 'Syntax' became a popular synonym for 'schoolmaster', according to Charles Hindley's glossary of current slang terms in his commentary on *The True History of Tom and Jerry* published in London in 1884.[5] The best known twentieth-century parallel to the popularity of an fictional character created by an artist probably would be Walt Disney's Mickey Mouse who was used by manufacturers to enhance the sales of their products. Doctor Syntax was clearly the pioneer of this practice. Hotten and others note the appearance of Syntax textile chintz, wigs, coats, hats, walking sticks and snuff boxes.

left fig. 11. Figurine of Doctor Syntax at York Races (compare to Plate 14).
centre fig. 12. Figurine of Doctor Syntax fiddling at the rural sports (compare to Plate 22).
right fig. 13. Figurine of Doctor Syntax in Paris.

Although locating examples of such souvenir Syntax apparel may challenge even the most avid and persistent of today's collectors, this is less true of other Syntax memorabilia, such as dinnerware and figurines. Gully notes blue-transfer dinnerware with Syntax illustrations produced in the early 1820s by the Staffordshire manufacturing firm, Clewes of Cobridge. An interesting article by Stanley Fisher provides several examples made in the Chamberlain factory in Worcester (and now in the collection of Mr. H. J. Lewis).[6] Gully also notes the recent production of Syntax plates by the Adams Company subsidiary of Wedgwood.

Of particular interest to collectors will be an article in *The Illustrated London News* from 1934 on porcelain Syntax figurines produced by the Derby factory in the early nineteenth century and produced, along with various forgeries, throughout the century.[7] Although some of the figurines depict scenes from imitations of the original Tours, such as the Paris tour, the examples illustrated here are from the original Tours for comparison to the corresponding plates (fig. 11 with Plate 14 and fig. 12 with Plate 22) and one from the *Doctor Syntax in Paris* imitation of the Doctor arriving at Calais with his hat firmly tied down (fig. 13).

To conclude this chapter on the influence of Doctor Syntax, brief comment should be made about the numerous unpublished Rowlandson drawings which, for various reasons, never found their way into the Tours. These, as with other works by this prolific artist, are mainly in museum or private collections. A proper appreciation of Rowlandson's colour requires a study of the original works and collectors of the Syntax books and prints may wish to visit the collections of The Huntington Museum in California and the Pierpont Morgan Library in New York, as well as the Victoria and Albert Museum in London, three of the many institutions that hold works by Rowlandson. In addition to Gully's list of locations holding unpublished Syntax drawings, I recommend Robert Wark's *Drawings by Thomas Rowlandson in the Huntington Collection* and Martin Hardie's illustrated article 'The Tours of Doctor Syntax: Rowlandson's Unpublished Illustrations' in *Connoisseur* for some well-reproduced examples.[8] I have chosen two as samples: 'Dr. Syntax and the Stranded Whale' (fig. 14) and 'Dr. Syntax Dining in the Lake' (fig. 15), both of which suggest interesting visual narrative but which, for various reasons, were never published.

Rowlandson's unique ability to tell a story through a single illustration or an episodic sequence, combined with the innovations of George Woodward and Henry Bunbury, provided an antecedent for such illustrated comic magazines as the long-lived *Punch* and later magazines and newspapers carrying comic strips, now the stock-in-trade of twentieth century newspapers and comic books. Some of

Fig. 14. Unpublished drawing of Doctor Syntax and the stranded whale.

Fig. 15. Unpublished drawing of Doctor Syntax dining in the lake.

Rowlandson's use of stock subjects, which were popular in his day—such as sex and marriage; satirical treatment of professional pomposity in medicine, law, and religion; poking fun at human foibles whether found in city or rural life; and adventures of comic characters which keep the reader's attention from episode to episode—have all found their way into the numerous newspapers and magazines that exist now. It seems appropriate that Doctor Syntax and his creator should be recognised once again for their considerable impact on our lives today.

CHAPTER FOUR

FURTHER STUDY AND COLLECTING

A S THE PREVIOUS CHAPTER HAS SHOWN, THERE WAS A REMARKABLE demand for and production of Syntax-related publications and other goods during the nineteenth century. Those interested in collecting should be encouraged, therefore, in knowing that Doctor Syntax books and prints are still available to patient and persistent seekers.

Although reprints of the three Tours ceased to appear in the twentieth century, the earlier editions of the books, the prints and other memorabilia had apparently continued to attract new audiences. For example, in his article on Rowlandson's unpublished Syntax drawings, Martin Hardie notes that "during the last few years" the popularity of books with coloured illustrations, such as the Doctor Syntax series, has increased and "for a set of the three Tours of Dr. Syntax, the collector must be prepared to pay from ten to fifteen pounds".[1] A collector in the 1990s should be prepared to pay about the same for a single print.

In 1934, in an *Illustrated London News* article on collecting Syntaxiana, Frank Davis writes that "most people are acquainted with the name of Dr. Syntax, but not many would care to answer an examination on his life and adventures".[2] And as late as 1951, Stanley Fisher in an *Apollo* article on porcelain Doctor Syntax jugs in a private collection writes, "Among [Rowlandson's] many creations, none is more enjoyed and appreciated nowadays than his famous Doctor Syntax".[3] While it may be true that Doctor Syntax remains best-known in his own country, one can find books and prints in America as well as in Britain. However, locating the porcelain pieces may present a challenge in either country.

A few places that have been helpful to this collector in locating prints include Lyons Ltd. in San Francisco, C. Dickens in Atlanta and Storey's Ltd., Quinto Book-shop and The Print Room, all in London. Doubtless, there are many more places, either favourites of other collectors, or those numerous out-of-the-way shops with unexpected 'finds' regardless of the country.

In examining prints, buyers must expect to find some differentiation in colouring, as well as other relatively minor features of the drawings. Although the ideal would be to come upon an available Rowlandson original drawing for the Syntax series, most of these are now in collections. The process following the artist's original design may be helpful to collectors. Here is Joseph Grego's description from his two-volume work on Rowlandson in 1880:

> A neat and carefully finished drawing of the original design was first prepared (these studies were afterwards purchased by Mr. Ackermann) and Rowlandson etched the outline sharply and clearly on the copper plate, an impression from the 'bitten-in' outline was printed on drawing-paper and the artist put in his shadows, modelling of forms and sketchy distance, with Indian ink, in the most delicate handling possible; the shadows were then copied in aquatint on the outlined plate, sometimes by the designer, but in most cases by an engraver who practised this particular branch, which a few experts were able to manipulate with considerable dexterity and nicety. Rowlandson next completed the colouring of his own Indian ink shaded impression in delicate tints, harmoniously selected; his sense of colour being of a rewned order as regarded the disposal tender shades agreeable to the eye . . . The tinted impression, which was intentionally finished with greater delicacy and elaboration than the artist generally displayed, served as a copy for imitation, which was handed to Mr. Ackermann's trained staff of colourists, the publisher finding constant employment for a number of clever persons whom he had educated expressly for this skilled employment.[4]

This was a brief but highly productive period of book illustration. Anonymous colourists, many of whom were women and children, produced hand-coloured aquatints. Anthony Gully has noted, "[the] colourists produced an incredible number of plates. *The Repository of Artist and Manufacture*, Ackermann's most successful periodical, rich with illustrations, arrived at a circulation of over 3,000 subscribers".[5] Ackermann published a large number of heavily-illustrated books during this period. However, this interesting but demanding process was soon to give way to industrial Victorian England's new engraving and lithography.

Before concluding this chapter with bibliographical listings of editions, translations and imitations of Doctor Syntax and a selected listing of studies dealing with Rowlandson, Combe, Ackermann and the Syntax collaboration, perhaps a few suggestions are in order on some variations for collecting the prints, assuming, of course, that not all collectors will be lucky enough to find modestly-priced early editions of the Tours with illustrations still intact. The numbers refer to the plates in this book.

1. Collecting paired prints. Sometimes these are contrasting scenes, an observation made by Ronald Paulson and expanded by Anthony Gully.

From Tour 1: Plates 5 and 6: 'Dr. Syntax Stopped by Highwaymen' and 'Dr. Syntax Bound to a Tree': and Plates 25 and 26: 'Dr. Syntax Reading His Tour' and 'Dr. Syntax Preaching'.

From Tour 2: Plates 33 and 34: 'Dr. Syntax Lamenting the Loss of His Wife' and 'Dr. Syntax at the Funeral of His Wife'; and Plates 42 and 43: 'Dr. Syntax Making His Will' (poking fun at doctors) and 'Dr. Syntax in a Court of Justice (poking fun at lawyers).

From Tour 3: Plates 79 and 80: 'Dr. Syntax In Danger' and 'The Funeral of Dr. Syntax' ; and Plates 66 and 67: 'The Harvest Home' (joys of country life) and 'The Garden Trio' (joys of city life).

2. Collecting other thematic scenes.

Plate 1 'The Rev. Dr. Syntax' and Plate 57 'Setting Out' provide a nice match on the theme of beginnings and endings, or preparation and action.

Plate 27 'Dr. Syntax and the Bookseller', Plate 29 'The Doctor's Dream', and Plate 53 'Dr. Syntax and the Bookseller' provide a pleasant trio on selling, buying and dreaming about books.

Scenes involving horses, horse racing and fox hunting (Plates 14, 15, 21, 46, 73, 76 and 77) reflect Rowlandson's interest in drawing horses and offer an interesting medley on Syntax's exploits with horses, his own and others'. Incidentally, a famous and successful race horse during the Victorian era was named 'Doctor Syntax', another indication of the touring cleric's popularity.

Plates on gaming, such as cards and billiards (Plates 64 and 68).

Plates on the joys of drinking (Plates 17 and 62)

Plates on Syntax as artist (Plates 13, 18, 19, 50 and 72)

Plates on Syntax as musician (Plates 22, 66 and 67)

Possible combinations are numerous just from the Three Tours alone.

Other collecting of individual prints from various editions of the Tours, from *Johnny Quæ Genus* and from other Syntax-related books are added possibilities. For help with this, a chronological list appears in Appendix One.

APPENDICES

EDITIONS, TRANSLATIONS, IMITATIONS AND RELATED BOOKS: A CHRONOLOGICAL LIST

May 1809–May 1811 'The Schoolmaster's Tour' in Ackermann's *Poetical Magazine*, featuring one or more Rowlandson drawings in each monthly issue.

1812   *The Tour of Doctor Syntax in Search of the Picturesque*. The first edition of the First Tour, with three new illustrations added to the *Poetical Magazine* group: (1) a frontispiece, (2) a title page and (3) 'The Doctor's Dream'.

1812   Second edition of the First Tour.

1813   Three more editions of the First Tour.

1815   The First Tour reissued; also a further reissue in 1817 and two more in 1819.

1815–1821 Numerous imitations, frequently using the Syntax name.

1815   *The Life of Napoleon, by Doctor Syntax*. London, 1815. With thirty engravings by George Cruikshank.

1815   *The Adventures of Doctor Comicus, In twelve cantos by a modern Syntax*. London [1815].

1820   *The Tour of Doctor Syntax Through London, or The Pleasures and Miseries of the Metropolis*. London: J. Johnson, 1820.

1820   *Doctor Syntax in Paris, or A Tour in Search of the Grotesque*. London: W. Wright, 1820.

1820   *The Tour of Doctor Prosody, in Search of the Antique and Picturesque, Through Scotland, the Hebrides, the Orkney and Shetland Isles*. London, Edinburgh and Glasgow, 1821.

1820   *The Second Tour of Doctor Syntax, in Search of Consolation* in eight instalments in *Poetical Magazine*, January to August 1820.

1820   *Second Tour* published in boards in late 1820.

1820   Danish translation of the First Tour published in Copenhagen. No illustrations.

1820   'Doctor Syntax in Search of a Wife'. Published in installments beginning in the same year as the Second Tour, in response to the growing popularity of Syntax. *Poetical Magazine*, November 1820 to May 1821.

1821   *Doctor Syntax in Search of a Wife.* (Hardbound.) Published by Ackermann, London.

1821   (Translation) *Le Don Quichotte Romantique, ou voyage du Docteur Syntaxe.* Paris: M. Gandais, 1821.

1821–22   *The History of Johnny Quae Genus, the Little Foundling of Doctor Syntax.* With verse by Combe, twenty-four engravings by Rowlandson and published by Ackermann in five parts dated 1821 and three dated 1822.

1822   (Translation) *Des Doktor Syntax Reise.* Berlin: Preuss, 1822.

1823   The First, Second and Third Tours are published in three separate miniature editions (3" x 6"). The miniatures underwent numerous reprints. This is also the year of Combe's death.

1827   Rowlandson dies.

1834   Ackermann dies.

1838   The First Tour, with new illustrations by 'Alfred Crowquill' (Alfred Henry Forrester) published in London by Methuen & Co. Reissued in 1865 and again in 1903 by Methuen & Co. in London and Appleton & Co. in New York.

1848   *Three Tours* published by C. Daly.

1855   *Three Tours* published by Nattali and Bond.

1868   *Three Tours*, with a Life of Combe by John Camden Hotten. Published by Chatto & Windus in London. Reprinted several times. Slightly revised new edition published in 1895.

1869   *Three Tours* published by Alexander Murry & Son.

1871   *Three Tours* published by Frederick Warne & Co.

1880s   During the 1880s, there were some American publications of the later editions, including one printing for free distribution by Warner's Proprietary Medicine Company in Chicago.

1903   Reprint of the Rowlandson-Combe-Ackermann originals by Methuen & Co.

THE HISTORY OF JOHNNY QUÆ GENUS
THE LITTLE FOUNDLING OF THE LATE DOCTOR SYNTAX
A POEM BY THE AUTHOR OF THE THREE TOURS
WITH TWENTY-FOUR COLOURED ILLUSTRATIONS BY THOMAS ROWLANDSON

1. Quæ Genus on his Journey to London.

2. Quæ Genus, in search of Service.

3. Quæ Genus reading to Sir Jeffery Gourmond.

4. Quæ Genus at Oxford.

5. Conflict between Quæ Genus & Lawyer Gripe-all.

6. Quæ Genus at a Sheep shearing.

7. Quæ Genus assisting a Traveller.

8. Quæ Genus in the Sports of the Kitchen.

9. Quæ Genus in the Service of Sir Jeffery Gourmand.

10. Quæ Genus with a Quack Doctor.

11. Quæ Genus with a Spendthrift.

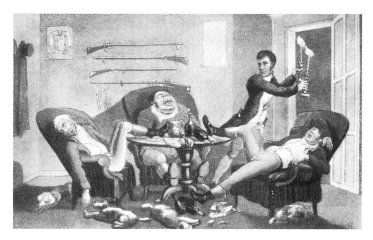

12. Quæ Genus attends on a Sporting Finale.

13. Quæ Genus in the Service of a Miser.

14. Quæ Genus & the Money Lenders.

15. Quæ Genus officiating at a Gaming Table.

16. Quæ Genus with a Portrait Painter.

17. Quæ Genus gives a Grand Party.

18. Quæ Genus interrupts a Tête a Tête.

19. Quæ Genus committed, with a riotous dancing Party, to the Watch-House.

20. Quæ Genus engaged with jovial friends; Or Who sings best?

21. The Party breaking up, and Quæ Genus breaking down.

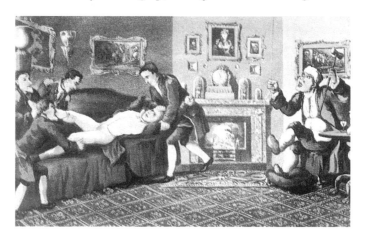

22. Quæ Genus turned out of a house which he mistakes for his own.

23. Quæ Genus & Creditors.

24. Quæ Genus discovers his Father.

NOTES

Chapter 1

1. The source for Gilpin's ideas, as well as examples of his sketches and paintings, is his *Three Essays: on Picturesque Beauty; on Picturesque Travel; and on Sketching Landscape*, first published in London in 1792 and later issued in an expanded third edition in 1808 with two added and illustrated essays on the principles and techniques Gilpin used in producing his drawings. Gilpin's picturesque drawings and Rowlandson's comic responses to some of them are discussed in chapter five of Anthony Gully's unpublished dissertation.
2. William Combe, *Letters to Marianne* (1823), p. vi.
3. Anthony Lacy Gully, 'Thomas Rowlandson's 'Doctor Syntax'', 1972, p. 80.
4. Ibid., pp. 93–113. The examples discussed by Gully include the books of William Gilpin. Rowlandson, himself a traveller, enjoys poking fun with humorous travel scenes, for example plates 13 and 18.
5. John Hayes, *Rowlandson: Watercolours and Drawings*, 1972, p.12.

Chapter 3

1. See Appendix One for further information about these editions. See also Gully 1972, pp. 160–61 and pp. 483–84, for further discussion.
2. From the Preface to *The History of Johnny Quæ Genus*, 1822 (preface written in May 1821).
3. Published by John Harris & Son in London, 1820.
4. *Doctor Syntax's Three Tours: In Search of the Picturesque, of Consolation and of a Wife* (London: Chatto & Windus, 1868 and 1895), p. xxvii.
5. Charles Hindley, *The True History of Tom and Jerry* (London, 1884), p. 207.
6. Stanley Fisher, 'Dr. Syntax on Porcelain', *Apollo* vol. 53 (1951), 43–46.
7. Frank Davis, *The Illustrated London News* (29 September 1934).
8. Robert R. Wark, *Drawings by Thomas Rowlandson in the Huntington Collection* (San Marino, California: Huntington Library, 1975); Martin Hardie, 'The Tours of Doctor Syntax: Rowlandson's Unpublished Illustrations', *Connoisseur*, vol. 18 (1907), pp. 215–19.

Chapter 4

1. Martin Hardie, 'The Tours of Doctor Syntax: Rowlandson's Unpublished Illustrations', *Connoisseur*, vol. 18 (1907), pp. 215–19.
2. Frank Davis, *The Illustrated London News* (29 September 1934).
3. Stanley W. Fisher, 'Dr. Syntax on Porcelain', *Apollo*, vol. 53 (1951), pp. 43–46.
4. Joseph Grego, *Thomas Rowlandson, The Caricaturist* (London: Chatto & Windus, 1880), vol. 1, pp. 33–34.
5. Gully 1972, p. 17, note 25.

SELECT BIBLIOGRAPHY

Sam Syntax's Description of the Cries of London as They are Daily Exhibited in the Streets. London: John Harris & Son, 1820.

Barbier, Carl. *William Gilpin: His Drawings, Teachings and Theory of the Picturesque*. Oxford, 1963.

Burke, W. J. 'Rudolph Ackermann, Promoter of Arts and Sciences,' New York: New York Public Library Publications, 1935.

Bury, Adrian. *Rowlandson Drawings*. London: Avalon, 1949.

Cole, Desmond. *Confessions of an Incurable Collector*. London, 1928.

Davis, Frank. 'A Page for Collectors: A Rowlandson Character in Porcelain.' *Illustrated London News*, CLXXXV (1934), pp. 486.

Falk, Bernard. *Thomas Rowlandson: His Life and Art*. London: Hutchinson,[1949].

Fisher, Stanley W. 'Dr. Syntax on Porcelain'. *Apollo*, vol. 53 (1951), pp. 43–46.

Gilpin, William. *Three Essays: on Picturesque Beauty; on Picturesque Travel; and on Sketching Landscapes*. London, 1792.

Grego, Joseph. *Thomas Rowlandson, the Caricaturist*. 2 vols. London, 1880.

Gully, Anthony Lacy. 'Thomas Rowlandson's 'Doctor Syntax'.' Unpublished Ph.D. dissertation for Stanford University, 1972.

Hamilton, Harlan. *Doctor Syntax, a Silhouette of William Combe, Esq*. London: Chatto & Windus, 1969.

Hardie, Martin. 'The Tours of Doctor Syntax: Rowlandson's Unpublished Illustrations'. *Connoisseur*, vol. 18 (1907), pp. 215–19.

Hayes, John. *Rowlandson: Watercolours and Drawings*. London: Phaidon, 1972.

Johnson, A. F. 'Rudolf Ackermann and Thomas Rowlandson'. *Penrose's Annual*, vol. 38 (1935) pp. 41–43.

Oppe, Paul. *Thomas Rowlandson, His Drawings and Watercolours*. London: *Studio*, 1923.

Paulson, Ronald. *Rowlandson: A New Interpretation*. London: Studio Vista,1972.

Rienaecker, Victor. 'Rowlandson's Prints and Print Collectors'. *Print Collectors Quarterly*, (1932) pp. 11–30.

Roberts, J. F. A. *William Gilpin on Picturesque Beauty*. Cambridge: Cambridge University Press, 1944.

Sabin, F. Catalogues to exhibitions at the Sabin Gallery, London, for 1933, 1938 and 1948.

Sitwell, Osbert. *Thomas Rowlandson*. In the *Famous Watercolour Painters* series. London, 1929.

Templeman, D. *The Life and Work of William Gilpin*. Urbana: University of Illinois Press, 1939.

Wark, Robert R. *Rowlandson's Drawings for a Tour in a Post Chaise*. San Marino, California: Huntington Library and Art Gallery, 1964.

——. *Rowlandson's Drawings for the English Dance of Death*. San Marino, California: Huntington Library and Art Gallery, 1966.

——. *Drawings by Thomas Rowlandson in the Huntington Collection*. San Marino, California: Huntington Library, 1975.

Selected List of Collections of Original Rowlandson Drawings related to Doctor Syntax

UNITED KINGDOM

1. The Victoria and Albert Museum, London (The Dyce Collection).
2. The Courtauld Institute of Art, London (The Witt Collection).
3. Harrogate Public Library, Yorkshire.
4. The British Museum, London.
5. The Arts Council of Great Britain (Gilbert Davis Collection).

UNITED STATES OF AMERICA

1. The Huntingdon Library and Art Gallery, San Marino, California.
2. The Pierpoint Morgan Library, New York.
3. New York City Public Library (The Berg Collection).
4. The Boston Museum of Fine Arts.
5. Harvard University (The Widener Collection).

INDEX OF NAMES